Windows of Night

by Charles Williams

the apocryphile press
BERKELEY, CA
www.apocryphile.org

apocryphile press
BERKELEY, CA

Apocryphile Press
1700 Shattuck Ave #81
Berkeley, CA 94709
www.apocryphile.org

First published by Oxford University Press, 1925.
First Apocryphile edition, 2007.

For sale in the USA only. Sales prohibited in the UK.
Printed in the United States of America.

ISBN 1-933993-35-9

CERTAIN of these poems have appeared in *Blackfriars*, the *London Mercury*, the *New Witness*, the *Monthly Paper* of St. Silas-the-Martyr, Kentish Town, and in two anthologies—Mr. W. K. Seymour's *Miscellany of Poetry*, *1920–2*, and Mr. V. H. Collins's *Poems of Home and Overseas*. One poem (*The Wars of the Roses*) had its origin in a misreading of a poem by Mr. A. S. Cripps, *Les Belles Roses sans Merci*. Another (the first of the Sonnets *In Time of Danger*) contains a simile which has been used by Mr. A. E. Housman in his *Last Poems*, but since it was written before his book appeared, any removal or alteration would seem to imply an impossible claim to equality.

CONTENTS

CONTENTS

CONTENTS vii

A MEDITATION ON THE THREE THEOLOGICAL
  VIRTUES 128
FOR A PICTURE 129
ON MY FRIENDS COMING TO HEAR ME LECTURE 130
ON ARRIVING ANYWHERE IN TIME FOR ANYTHING . 131
CHRISTMAS 132
EASTER 134
SAINT MICHAEL 135
SAINT MARY MAGDALENE 136
SAINT STEPHEN 138
ON THE SANCTISSIMUM (i) THE REAL PRESENCE 140
                    (ii) CRUX MUNDI . . 141
                   (iii) AT COMMUNION . 142
                   (iv) AT A PROCESSION . 143
SATISFACTION 144
TO A PUBLISHER 145
LAST THOUGHTS BEFORE SLEEP 152

Prelude

(To H. S. M.)

WHEN from the house where I was nursed
　　Into the outer world I first
　With doubtful footing went,
I saw in a bewildered earth
Nor nights of peace nor days of mirth
　Nor twilights of content.

All the unhappiness of youth
I knew, and knew it less than truth,
　And felt beneath me move
The quaking ground whereon I trod,
Spoiling the towers of every god,
　And all the doors of love.

I saw the blinding tyrants smite
Their serving-folk with death or night
　For avarice or whim ;
The dancing heavens go lightly by
Above the plague pits, huddled high
　With corpses to the brim.

I saw, above all purpose set,
The fitful poised Almighty threat
　Float sadly in the air,
Which, though but few it seemed to strike
With madness, cancer, and their like,
　Yet taught to all despair.

I knew the last fear—lest there hid
In Death's unopened pyramid
   Only Life's self abhorred :
But O amid such darkening gloom
What fantasy decreed my doom
   Beneath a courteous lord ?

All things I feared—and lo on me
The world's accustomed irony,
   Grown swiftly gracious, smiled :
Among the starving I was fed,
Into security was led,
   And guarded from the wild.

Yet, for all favours of its past,
How should I trust Life's grace to last?
   Only, the chance of ill
More distant and more doubtful runs
Afar from me, since all my suns
   Are blest with your goodwill.

And what more joys, what friendships new,
Had happily their source in you !
   As when we left the town,
And shy and laughing and amazed
To hear myself by strangers praised,
   We took the road to Downe :

As London, my own city, known
For a mere torment of great stone
  By many a wandering wit,
Re-risen for me, stood in the void
Of my desire, and was enjoyed,
    For you were part of it.

In one same spring your name and hers,
The world's and heaven's best messengers,
  Smote first my careless ears :
Who knew not then what springs should build
About me, from those names fulfilled,
    A shelter for my years.

Those names fulfilled !—Of the last End,
The Mystery that hath for friend
  All governments of peace,
What pious dream hath more of fame
Than each admired prophetic name,
    Sounding it without cease?

Faint though I fall in ways of ill,
I see the shining glory still
  In the world's fair employ,
Creation marvellously wrought
To one sole multitudinous thought,
    The Day, the Morning Joy.

And bitter though within me hate
Wars with inexorable Fate,
  To wreck its rich delight,
I know the hinted close of dawn,
The quenched activities withdrawn,
  The Evening Joy, the Night.

But her a hundred sonnets praise,
And all the friends who tread my ways
  Have each their share of song ;
Yet, sir, my world must lack its due
Accomplishment, except to you
  Some period may belong.

Poets by generations count
Their lives, and sum the full amount
  In centuries ; but I,
Whom no kind Muse hath brought to name
Within the sanctuary of Fame,
  Before my death must die.

On many a mightier shield than mine
Your quartered arms shall they design
  Who keep the heraldic scrolls
Of Art ; but though the future paints
You in the list of their All Saints,
  You will not scorn All Souls ?

Then, maugre what the wise allow,
Under your titles be I now
   Of this small freehold seised ;
And let me to my doubtful heart
Profess a virtue in my art,
    For you were sometimes pleased.

These meditations, since your care
Sustains unharmed my household stair,
   And the peace where they grow,
Take, the poor symbols of your due ;
All verse, and more than verse, to you,
    With her and God, I owe.

Sleep

NOW industry is ended; now, kind sleep,
  Only be pleased to be not overswift,
But let our loosed and drowsy bodies keep
  A little taste of exile; slowly sift
Night's heavier from the airy thoughts of day,
  And at the point of our surrender make
Some new, delicious, ever-shorter stay;
  Slowly to sleep is good, swiftly to wake.
Ah! coveted Joy, too absolute in content
  To be exchanged for immortality,
How dost thou lure us from our late consent
  And our night prayers to light and ecstasy,
Tempting us now, with our last waking breath,
To ask no more, but only this, of death.

The Window

PUT out the candles, friend, while I unclose
  The window of our thought upon the night,
 Time, and the world, where London, light by light,
  Twinkles away into an unknown end
And darkness at the edge of Being flows ;
 Upon the slope, which at this sill begins
 But there is lost in what black origins !
  Put out the lights, put out the candles, friend :
No gleam upon the guessed horizon throws
 Any small flaming wick of faith or hope,
 For studies meet, nor on the ragged slope,
Which here the intent Imagination knows.

Out of the black and vacant heaven looks down
 An everlasting silence, here touched white
 With borrowed flame to the fantastic site
  Of mirrored cities and reflected streets.
Turn, turn your eyes ! this is man's topmost town,
 Close-set beneath us : there is Thames, and here,
 Where the glow gathers deepest, Westminster ;
  District on district thrust, while each repeats
Some huge word man's devising mind hath known,
 Some station upon his long toil, which we
 Here dimly from his first beginning see,
But not his end, nor whereby helped or thrown.

The window of our nature opens : see,
    In the vast vision of our conscious mind,
    A living mud bubbles into mankind
        Momently, and each moment from the mud
Shapes yet another surge of anarchy.
    Life wakes and heaves and in a babble of cries
    Swarms out of earth a little, and so dies
        And is swallowed under life ; what streaks of blood
Gleam under us here !   But soon an end shall be,
    For now the fires of other labourers flare
    Along sides till now unseen, and all men share
A final sorrow and sad certainty.

Now all draws inward ; now where once was night,
    Shaken with fabulous and impalpable wings
    Of phoenix, roc, or bird-like angel, springs
        The fiery line of knowledge ; see, the last
Far corner flickers into doubtful light ;
    All nears to all ! short space remains to span
    Of the unknown leagues that for so long were man,—
        Leagues of the vast unsearchable world, the vast
Unsearchable soul, now narrow into sight,
    In one last thunder of confusion send
    Their joined adventure to its fatal end,
Achieve their work, and perish on its height.

But we ere then shall perish ; lo, this Year,
    This rising Hour which, level with our sill,
    Pantingly busy at Time's secular will,
        Builds up the huge waste-circled pyramid,
His single praise, memorial, and mere

Monstrosity of Being, whose wide base
Rests on the everlasting square of Space,
  In ancient and neglected darkness hid.
Upward the generations swarm, and here
  Their latest palpitations, thick and close,
  Beat where Time's self directs, raucous and gross,
Their sweat to lift it by this present tier.

Beneath them, lo the farther builders! they
  Who fashioned the huge side whereon we stand,
  City on city, land on shifting land,
    Beneath our busy thought sounding yet mute,
Whose reputable tasks did but obey
  One mastery with ours; dead fingers touch
  The foot that juts from our year's ledge, and clutch
    About our ankles; they no more dispute
Betwixt themselves for honour, to no fray
  Man's trumpet of Possession calls them now,
  But in our generation each can grow,
Preying on us who made them first our prey.

Under what overseers did they move!
  Who with new knowledge mortising the stair,
  Smoothing the level, seeking how and where
    The next great surge of Being should arise,
Were their chief governors, whether they rove
  Outer or inner worlds,—the Genoan
  Once, and once he who first made isled Japan
    Part of the world's mind, they who brought the skies
Into its range; Plato and who else hove
  Some mass of meditation up, long time
  Beyond the climbing level, or whose rhyme
Uttered the songs and secrets of man's love.

What songs ? What chants from shelf or coign of rest
  Largely inform with meaning our turmoil,
  Catching the note and rhythm of our toil ?
    Some sweetly praising, marvellously elate,
The stretched arm-muscles or the naked breast
  Of a near fellow ; others' wider song
  Makes credible purpose of our trial age-long,
    The unfinished apex, and all-ruling fate.
One only left the pyramid's peak unguessed,
  Our English greatest ; a few others see
  Dark truth,—the Roman wildly dead, and he
Of Wessex, wrack'd futility confessed.

For now we hear what long the loud slope hid,—
  So high this window opens on the past
  In all its broad decline,—we hear at last
    Song melting with its thousand epic tales
And heroes, Rama, Siegfried, Al Raschid,—
  Foam on a sea of sound,—into the whole
  Potent, impetuous, and upward roll.
    Into one roar the separate music fails ;
Which in its day so wonderfully amid
  The separate clamours rose, all hearers swung
  In mightier strain after each golden tongue,
Faster and fuller working as Time bid.

O what else wrought they whom our deep minds con ?
  Rumours which through our wisest spirit ran,
  Fabled and felt ; in whom content began ;
    Shapes where man to himself once named and knew
The loveliest lures in which Time ever shone ;

And the bright mist about the peak was fair
With mighty apparition shadowed there
    Of the Lord Buddha and such holy few :
For whose blest folk Time's self hath undergone
Transfiguration, and to saintlihood
Cheated with heavenly dreams, else by no rude
Earth's lust enticed nor the world's vision wan.

Through us their great but dying names are blown,
    Smothered with voices ; where long since they sank,
    Still boiling in an ever-restless bank,
        Our clay remembers them, so strong they were ;
But now their liveliest words are overgrown,
    Now since so near we climb unto the peak
    All that they prophesied we no more seek ;
        Their vanity of expectation here
Dissolves into oblivion ; the world's moan
    Shall mournfully remember them no more ;
    Far off those banks their heaving shall give o'er,
And the whole dead past harden into stone.

It is not past, it is not dead ! it moves,
    It stirs with life ; all that men were they are,
    Vastly and dimly visioned from afar
        Down the wide slope of Being ; tribes and hordes
Mingling and whelmed in their own herds and droves
    Pulse rhythmically through creation ; there,
    At our sight's end, beyond the lights, all share
        One common welter, cattle and their lords.
Among the horned, pointed, or flat heads moves
    The earliest rounded ; all one hunger sweeps
    Upward, each strives and falls and climbs and leaps
For his day's portion and his yearly loves.

Around and over them the great night flows ;
  The night of genesis, the fount of all
  Our life and height. What god, what animal,
    Therein was our first father, when the pit
Of space first held, running with melted snows,
  Perception ? What divine or bestial head
  Remembers us ? what hands or paws are spread
    Upon the mighty stair to clamber it ?
Feel we not how on our interior throes,
  Shaking the ladder of spaces and of times,
  This living and forgotten monster climbs,
Dragging the night behind him as he goes ?

Before whose coming what fear shakes the air,
  What portent ? Feel'st thou 'neath our topmost tread,
  Noisome and too much laden with its dead,
    The whole mound tremble ? Life that builded it
Faints in her task, and all the marvellous stair
  Time shall see crash ; the works begin to slide
  And cracks of chaos open on each side ;
    Thought, living, looks into the bottomless pit,
Shudders o'er precipices of despair,
  Shafts of destruction ; Being is torn apart,
  Feel'st thou the terror leaping in thy heart ?
All 's rent, all breaks, and Nothing is laid bare.

Shut down the window, light the candles, friend ;
  This way we lean o'er madness, this way lies
  Void where man's dying soul that never dies,
    Wholly forsaken, wholly unpursued,
Wholly unlured to any conscious end,

Drops in a sick and everlasting fall
Through ceaseless depth, by powers anarchical
   Blown but not stayed.   O let our flames renewed,
Our toil, our hope, our tenderness, befriend
   The encompassed mind against the encompassing
      gloom !
Here lies my Herrick, in the farther room
They are playing Grieg ; come in, let us attend.

Domesticity

IS it knowledge, is it knowledge only and fear
   Lest one chance of many should bring this body at
     last
To burning or drowning? or exile from its dear
Companions and instruments, locked in a prison cell?

Fear or more than fear? O Earth's body, what pain
Tightens the whole fine nervous web? what ache
In the torn bloody past twitches our brain?
Is it in the mind alone that memory lives?

Now when at morning the house turns round to the sun,
All the dead life that lay through the dark at the back of
     our minds
Stirs, and ghosts in the visible world have begun
Anew to occupy eyes left vacant by sleep.

Without and within sleep parts from the world in a moan
Of universal memory, presences dwelling alive
In the wrathful elements, victims whose hurt we condone
Using the means whereby they were brought to doom.

Naiads and pretty gnomes, where are you, and brave
Salamanders? when did our perishing fancy leave
Its early delight in hearth and spring and cave?
Or were you in truth no more than an antique dream?

No, no, you were; but races die : you died
When another people thronged the streams and groves,
Gay with no dances ; you ceased before the tide
Of mortal sorrow ; now you are seen no more.

Our colonies reached your lands; you too mankind
Seized for his vengeance first, and then by his pain;
You, to the hate which his gloomy heart designed,
Involuntarily, injuriously compelled.

One and indivisible, man, man whose whole power
Is drawn to the smallest act of his smallest child,
Man haunted by himself for ever, man lords you this hour.
Seek you some other country! gentles, farewell.

His purpose, his past, my doleful body shares,
Morning by morning accepting the terrible sun,
Bathing or lighting a fire or going downstairs
What old companions crowd us, see, in our first need!

Unseen, ineluctable, those whom Morgan's blades
Pricked from the ship's side, Margaret Wilson, or they
Of France and Couthon, the stripped and bound noyades,
Floating for ever wherever water flows.

Water's cool refreshment refreshed not them:
Cleansed we arise,—cleansed and the more defiled
By obscene currents of death no oblivion can stem
Or distil from the general river, clogged and unclean.

And when we set match to the fire, the small flames scorch
Something other than wood: what inaudible cry
Rends my dumb spirit! 'twas thus they put the torch
To Joan's fire or Du Moulay's,—thus? no, with this.

This has lit Ridley's candle, here Smithfield pours
A red glare outward: my silent lips shout with the mob
Where to-day in the West a screaming negro endures
The last pains of death, and my food is cooked at his fire.

You at least, my walls, are kind ; in this recess
Where the laden bookshelves from floor to ceiling rise,
Comforting evasions, here need I fear no distress,—
Though the depth is enough to hold a man bound to the
    wall ;

And my book weighs heavy as a stone, and the cornice
    expands
Into curves of Babylon or Oudh, and eyes glimmer there
Through the last gap left unfilled by the eunuchs' hands,
And I thrust the stone hastily in and turn and go.

Where? for the very wallpaper stares straight ahead,
Seeming neither to whisper nor wink but to speak all the
    time
How beneath it the mortar is bloodily streaked, and what
    dead
It hides.   To the nurseries or to the cellars? where?

Bars of cots and nurseries only renew
In the tender care of love a most bitter care
To hold Bajazet safe, Buchan, or La Balue ;
Soft the bars rustle together and thus they say :

' Hold fast, brother, fast : though little fingers
Seem to clasp us a ghostly hand is there,
Clutching us over them, and between us lingers
A ragged shape and shuffling feet of despair.'

And beyond the steps to our cellars, when down we steal,
A door opens on darkness,—we almost tread
On the dying prisoners, lice-eaten, whom the Bastille
Held or the Tower or the Tullianum : one turn—

And lo through a secret chink between time and space
We shall come out afar in the Cocytëan South,
Lost for ever, turning a haggard face
On Tasman's rocks or the gunboat-guarded Bay.

Immortal foundations! unopened dungeons! here still
Hate steams like a pestilence upward, though far above
They build the millennium in storied peace and goodwill,
And men walk civilly,—but there they shall not forget;

They shall not forget the slain; they shall not awake
Or lie down in joy, but all their delicate lives
They, unforgiven, shall loathe for these others' sake,
Having no house to inhabit but this of our dead.

Prisoners

PRISONERS, where'er in bitter cells and small
  To-night you watch or sleep the hours away,
 Till the beginning of no hopeful day
Maps out your angry and steel-latticed wall,
Have mercy on me, for whose sake you are thrall
 To what man knows of fear, and are the prey
 Of the general mind, which slays you lest it slay,
And, lest it rob, robs you—and so with all.

By you against her citizens the land
  Protects herself: what each one singly would,
   The commonwealth of all hates, and for fear
Of her own lusts hath clutched you with rough hand;
  By you against herself protects her good,
   On you inflicts what I and all should bear.

The Two Domes

WHAT are those domes? *you asked in Clerkenwell ;*
       And I : One is the Old Bailey and one Saint
   Paul's,
Sitting up there like the broken halves of the shell
Of the egg of life, whose overspilt yolk we are.

Justice is perched on one, with her sword and scales,
And over her shoulder the ancient commentary,
The cross, in huge silence that neither hopes nor rails,
Peeps,—all judgement's ironical overthrow.

All wisdom, all might, watchfulness, meditation,
Fixed Law—the changeless, throned, perpetual judges,
Unfixed Opinion—the juries in congregation
Out of the mass, into the mass dissolving ;

All is overwatched by that vast and still
Quiet of the Cross, into its silence
Drawing the silence of corridors that fill
Morn by morn with speechless men in our prisons :

Speechless there by man's rule as once without speech
In the dock, because no word, however they sought
In agony and haste, because no thought could reach
To their central secret, the innermost unknown motive :

The unknown motive, the common truth of all lives,
Lost somewhere between those domes, the fearful cross,
The fearful justice ! O impotent law that strives
To pierce the guilty heart, and never finds it !

If judges some day having uttered their judgement arose
And themselves in the doomed man's stead were drawn
    to the bitter
Torment of prison or death—would that cure the woes
We suffer, and quench the unquenchable fiery pang?

Not for love's sake—leave that to a god!
Not for love but only to bring the irrational in!
Madness might wander where sanity never trod
And find the secret, and strike the irony dumb;

Strike out the cruel cross that calls us to heed
How the guilty suffer for us the guilty,—how we
Do righteously, judging rightly, but in the deed
Lose something we do not know, and lose it for ever.

Two equal bits of a dry hard brittle shell
With the yolk all spilt, the yolk that was life therein;
These are the domes you saw from Clerkenwell,
This is the deep unhappiness of our race.

To a Modern Poet

NOBLEST among the spirits that deny,
   Now when man's mind, so long time the stars
     drudge
  And scavenger of destiny, is made judge
O'er his futurity, can thy gaze espy,
Down the not-infinite slope of prophecy,
   The released generations, with less grudge
   For thwarted joy, now lightlier forward trudge,
Framing their will and choice wholly to die?

In you our vast conspiracy began
   First to be published to itself, and press
     To its completion, now through year on year
     Strengthening refusal, quelling all love and fear
   With love of the hour when absolute Nothingness
Shall quench the epoch and the grief of Man.

The Choice

WHEN I was weary
  And sick and poor,
Christ and Antichrist
  Came to my door,—
Baal of the flies
  From his marshy sell
And from the high hills
  Immanuel,
Each with a promise,
  Each for a guide,
Since amid falling walls
  I might no more abide.

' Here is drink to comfort,
  To ease, to bid arise,
To strengthen for thy journey,'
  Quoth Baal of the flies.
' Since thou canst dwell no more
  In thy wrecked abode,
Come, and ere thou goest
  On an infinite road,
Prove all thy heart's content
  With me for an hour,
Ere thou travel forward
  In comfortable power.'

' Here is drink for promise,'
  Quoth Immanuel,
' Of that which shall await thee
  In the holy well
At the joyous heavenly end
  Of an infinite way.
Since thou canst dwell no more
  In this wrecked To-day,
Come, and when the journey
  At last is overspent
Thou with me shalt understand
  All thy content.'

Then I fell before them,
  Crying : ' Ah my lords,
Who am I to compass
  Such immortal words ?
Is thy satisfaction
  Of such full avail
It can give me longing,
  O my master Baal,
For any moment
  Of any life at all
In the melancholy shadows
  That about thee fall ?
Not for thy temptations
  From heaven did I flee !
Talk thou with thy lovers
  Lord, depart from me !

‘ Nor, though not by Satan
    Shall my drink be spiced,
Dare I touch thy goblet,
    O my master Christ !
Have I ever prayed thee
    To be among thy saints,
At whose crucifixion
    My poor soul faints ?
Thou with peaks and chasms
    Ere the long way end,
Art thou that Forgetfulness
    I would have for friend ?
Not to find thy martyrdom
    Have I fled from hell ;
Thou hast many heroes,
    Bid me farewell ! ’

Low I fell before them,
    Crying : ‘ Ah my lords,
Who am I to compass
    Your immortal words ?
This have all things taught me,
    To desire no more
Than to be the dust again
    That I was before !
But who of all the high gods
    In heaven or hell
Hath such a draught as I would buy,
    Hath such draught to sell ? ’

Gnostic Apologue on the Parable of the Talents

ANOTHER servant, as they tell,
  Had chaffered long and bargained well,
Had speculated here and there
And watched the market-price with care,
And brought when judgement was begun
Ten talents back instead of one.

He came, and as he neared the hall
His thoughts ran backward over all
His toil : ' The worry that I've spent
Over house-property and rent,
And all the lengthy in-and-out
By which my gain was brought about !
If in the end my lord should ask
What gifts we covet for our task,
A little house shall be my prayer,
My freedom then, and if I dare
A pension ; last, only that he
Will never more remember me.
I couldn't stand another year
Of agitated hope and fear.'

c

He came, and as he neared the hall
He heard the sudden trumpets call,
Heard shouting and a rush of feet,
And cars and horses in the street ;
A crowd poured by him ; vivas ran
Through house and road, and in the van
Of all the tumult went the man
For whom the trumpets sounded : he,
Clothed in rich robes of dignity,
Paced slowly by our servant's eyes,
Who knew him, much to his surprise,
Another servant and his friend—
How brought unto this royal end?

He paused, he asked ; reply was brief
And multitudinous : ' He is chief
Now of ten townships ; our great lord
Lifts him thereto for meet reward
Of vantage gained and profit won—
Ten silver talents brought for one !
Ten talents brought, ten cities hail
Their master.'
                He began to quail :
' Ten cities' trouble for reward !
Ten markets hailing me for lord
When barely to be known in one
Left me by worry half-undone !
Ten crowds, ten thousand problems, ten
Shouting and hurrying gulfs of men ! . . .'

He paused, looked round, took breath,—and fled.
His lord for long supposed him dead,
Until one day by parcel post
Came back the talent he had lost
With other nine—a little note,
Undated, with no place to quote :
' I bore my labour, but, O lord,
I could not stomach the reward ! '

A Cup of Water

WHEN you awoke in the night and asked for water,
  Drank, and gave me the glass, and to sleep returned,
Little you knew, O Christendom's fairest daughter !
  On whose errand I ran, whose smile I earned.

Wakeful long had I lain while round about me
  Whistled the winds of the world with all their wrongs ;
Cold were the skies within and the skies without me
  Cold, and my brain sighed over its dying songs.

Flat was the earth, and westward was Ireland with
        burning
  Homes and America farther with burning men,
And out to the east were marching hosts returning
  From a dream of peace to smite each other again.

Through twisted ends of the world, in Korean cities,
  Serpents of Tyranny coiled with poisonous breaths,
And hard at home with the snow over frozen Pities
  Spun loud and louder the dance of fantastical Deaths.

And over the plain I looked on my Mother riding,
  Christendom, mighty and lovely, with naked blade,
Nation from nation and heart from heart dividing,
  Mocking with bitter words at her sons afraid.

High she rode, and beyond her, stripped of possession,
  Sages and heroes and prophets, a line of flame
Beating the world, and all who made her their profession,
  As Freedom, as Peace, or in any defeated name.

But I—poor wretch !—sought vainly around for shelter,
  Some hole to creep in,—too weak to ride with the
      strong,
Doomed to be trampled and lost in the bloody welter,
  Fleeing her wrathful eyes and her mouth of song.

Then waking, you asked for water ; with tender laughter
  I rose and served your need, and then couched again
Expecting the storm ; and lo of a sudden thereafter
  Were darkness and freedom, peace and an end to pain.

Slumber was there, and Love, and an end to thinking ;
  Only I saw, remote and far in the night,
Our mother Christendom pausing from war and drinking
  A cup of water,—and sleep came down on the sight.

Night Poems

I

OF all the hours what hour is best
But that which draws us both to rest?

And next, when early rumours shake
Our sleepiness and bid us wake:

For then the high delights that show
In our day's progress to and fro,—

And from some deep interior part
As if in sudden wrath do start

To be so long forgotten, and
Nimbly transmute a cheek or hand

Into a bright eternal thing,
A landmark on our wayfaring,—

Invisibly do us possess:
The wisdom that in wakefulness

Is by Imagination seen
Now in this soft betwixt-between

Flows through our limbs; eternity
Breathes at the lattices; and we,

Lightly together folded, prove
The immortal friendliness of love ;

When, last or first, the instinctive kiss
Reminds us what long privacies

Of night and of repose were known,
Preludes to this communion

Of peace, within whose waves we are
Far-borne and drawn again from far,

Filled with the happy, silent, deep
Potentialities of sleep.

II

Ille

AGAIN in a still peace, in clear
  Contentment, our twined souls abide,
While all about us, far and near,
  Entangled worlds of being slide.

Illa

If, dear my lord, on some dark day
  Fate and the world our love destroy,
Shall we not think of this and say :
  ' What times were ours ! and O what joy ! '

Ille

How oft from these delicious springs
  Of health that promise seems to fly
Before us, yet no darkness brings
  Its trial and redemption nigh !

Illa

Clasp me more close ! if time shall fret
  Our cords of joy to breaking strands,
We may our plighted tongues forget
  But not these kissed and clasping hands.

Ille

How marvellously did Love bless
  My early prayers, but framed anew !
I begged from him forgetfulness ;
  He gave forgetfulness—in you.

Illa

Alas ! what praise is this I hear ?
  Now am I worth no lovelier fame
From my best poet ? then forbear,
  I will not own so dull a name !

Ille

My fair Oblivion, be content !
  Is it a small thing that your bright
And unperturbed arbitrament
  Resolves my trouble out of sight ?

Illa

Not such repose was promised me
  In those blind moments when my blood,
Helpless as in the storm the sea,
  First leapt to your near neighbourhood.

Ille

Stilled it not to a sunnier mirth
  Thereafter ? as in me, who feel
About the deadly wound of birth
  Your hidden consolation steal.

Illa

Wounds though I suffer, let me move
  Ever in jeopardy and strife,
Until, beneath the wrath of love
  Broken, you nurse me back to life.

Ille

Since first one starry moment drew
　　Our too-long parted spirits nigh,
Time sinks at my arrest : in you
　　To all the world I seem to die.

Illa

But when on me arose that star
　　From its serene intensity
What ardour smote me ! lo, the scar
　　Red on my heart possesses me.

Ille

Joy bring your utmost hope to pass !
　　But if that wild flight touch the sky,
Think that, in me reposed, it has
　　A double strength of speed thereby !

Illa

Nor are your wars, O true and dear,
　　Less glorious that they seem to be
Dim raids upon the far frontier
　　Of an entire tranquillity.

Ille

Thus you, asleep in me, shall vaunt
　　Your courage ; I, asleep in you,
Shall satisfy that deeper want
　　Endured by all, breathed by how few !

III

MICHAL, what wealth of kisses do I owe,
   Dropt on my head when it in sleep is yours
And in oblivious comfort cannot know
   Through what soft word or touch your passion pours !
Must this new world the pattern of the old
   Repeat, with waste of beauty and delight,
My loveliest blessings still to me untold
   And even by you forgotten with the night ?
O no, they all are caught and gathered up,
   Most precious and enduring, and my own,
Pressed in the darkling contents of that cup
   Which I shall drink when all things are made known,
And without breaking then my heart endures
To bear the fullness of your *I am yours !*

To Michal : On Bringing her Breakfast in Bed

'I have been at the buttery in the land of the Trinity.'—*Taliessin*.

HERE come I from the buttery
   In the land of the Trinity.
With a new day's new supplies :
Open, Fair, those sacred eyes
On these rolls and fruit and tea,
All in order decently
Set upon a fair white cloth.
While a weight (too deep for sloth)
Held you on your pillows fast
Till all weariness had past
Your fresh beauty, I was up
With my platter and my cup,
Up and out beside the hatch
Which the early Hours unlatch,
Out beside the grills and gates
Where the world at morning waits
And tiptoeing just can see
The broad lands of the Trinity.

From these Northern heights went I
With an English company,—
Men and maids and mistresses :
A rare riot of degrees !—
Some, awaking earlier,
With the Easterns nourished were ;

Some in sleep delay advent
Till the Western continent
Surges there for food ; but we,
Timely waking timelessly,
Somewhere between six and seven
Halted at the bars of heaven ;
O what chatter filled the air !
None saw any other there,
Yet through London and our land
Called and answered all the band ;
Silently and surely called
To that house, by Nature walled,
Gated fast, till our desire
Saw the gate-pillars afire.
Many deputies have they
Who prepare our food each day,
But themselves have place behind
Each subordinated mind ;
Chiefly they direct the power
Grinds the corn to baking flour,
Milks the cow or crisps the tea.
O that heavenly industry !
Through the gates, with fires that burn,
Peeping down, could we discern
The Three Wise Masters ; of them one
Drew the bread when it was done,
Kept the blazing fires alight ;
One, dividing each his right
Lot and portion, so began
The great daily task of man,

Or with eyes of laughter kept
Shares aside for those who slept ;
One amidst our clusters rude
Taught civility, subdued
Greed in us, and (so to share
The work) was here and everywhere.
In and out the buttery
Worked the joyous Trinity.

(Them you saw not,—nor the wide
Flocks and droves that strayed beside
That dire house, that gate of dread !
Must their guiltless blood be shed,
And our comfort still prefer
That long morning massacre ?
Is not fruit of every kind,
Grapes, bananas, here to find,
Apples, watercresses, figs ?
Hath the Lord no care for pigs ?

Fear not, sweet ; those cloudy lids
Rise on naught that ruth forbids.
Later, when the sun is high
And our heavier minds descry
All the price that all things pay
For their sight of this pale day,
You shall know what Death informs
That land's lurid noon of storms.
In a lighter-darker hour
You shall feel a tempest lour ;
Dying, feed on death ; but now,
Innocent and joyous, grow

In waking on a scatheless show !
You who love the legend told
How Gautama once of old,
Meeting, ere his Buddha-birth,
A tigress, in a year of dearth,
Her and her young cubs to save
His thrice-sacred body gave !)

Backward from those gates, that burned
With the morning's fires, we turned ;
Furnished with full dish and can,
Each to his own doorway ran
In our colony ; while fade,
In the soul's remoter shade,
The high pastures, the dark sea,
The cornlands of the Trinity.
Fades their singing speed, the bright,
Quick, and curious delight
Of those channels, moors and hills,
To my tender duty stills,
Who at our own board prepare,
Sweet, for you the finer share.
Morn in you and morn without
Now anew are come about
To their high conjunction ; ease
Now those dainty limbs can please
But a little more—O wake
And behold me for your sake
Coming from the buttery
In the land of the Trinity.

Abroad

HEART, heart,
  What of thy joy,
So soft, so secret, so without cloy,
It lies forgotten
Unless thou cry,
Loud, unceasing, ' How joyous am I ! '

Heart, look round,
And see, see, see,
What chances to all and O to thee !
As yon twain go
In love's delight,
'Tis love, 'tis love, sets thy days right.

See with what joy
They meet, they part,
And watch, O watch, neglectful heart,
The farthest turn
Of utter peace
Which is tidal ebb of joy's increase.

Think, O heart,
All thou canst see
Of them is a witness again to thee ;
Thou hast their cause,
Thou hast their end,
Thou hast the sure passion of thy friend.

Gaze no more,
Think all of thee
Is apt as they to felicity ;
Delight does them
And thee employ :
Heart, how full is thy heart of joy !

Courtesy

IN the beginning of time
　　When, mingling night and day in your slender youth,
Sole created being
To move on creation, its sovereign meaning and mistress,—
When you came, dusky and brilliant,
And paused to greet me
(Me, also a god being your opposite and equal),
In the beginning first I knew that I loved
When it seemed so foolish, so needless,
So many heart-beats went by
Before I remembered that, in the world of phenomena,
One should always—and I to you, O absurdity !—
On meeting a lady, instinctively raise one's hat.

The Solution

PERFECTION
Is a quality impossible of attribution
To any created being ;
Imperfection
Is a quality impossible of attribution,
Fairest, to you ;
I suppose, therefore,
That your percentage of perfection
Is ninety-nine decimal nine recurring.

Theobalds' Road

THERE must be many Theobalds' Roads in the
   universe;
Images of images; almost, not quite, identical;
A little above, a little below, slanting across, here but
   not quite here;
Visible, tangible—but to me invisible, intangible.

I look for her hat: I wait, she has not come.
It is hardly time indeed, and it's pleasant to wait;
But a little laughter sounds in my mind—a stranger
Laughing there: ' You fool, she's waiting already.

' Time has many turnings, and Time and Space
Multiply infinitely between them this crowded world.
By mere chance she, coming out of the house to-day,
Just where two were co-incident, entered the other.

' You can wait as long as you like, you will never meet her.
She is gone for ever, as you from that other world
Where she now is waiting have vanished,—unless here-
   after
Some shock may hurl you across into that world's reckon-
   ing.

' There—twenty years hence or thirty, who knows how
    long ?—
Again you shall meet, unhappy, desolate, old ;
You, unknowingly translated, shall see a face
Where something moves that moved long since in your
    mind.

' It shall be there the only familiar thing
After those years' long absence : if she shall know you
What will she say or do ? . . . But as for the doctors,
They may call it loss of memory, they may call it madness.'

Antichrist

WHY seems your cheek so pale, young man,
   Why look your eyes so wild,
Within these walks of happy Love,
   So still and undefiled?

Fear you the Adversary here
   Who with us squires will fight?
'Tis Love, 'tis Love, that tries us so
   To prove us men of might.

Or have you in some secret coign
   With your Accuser met?
Ah, then those eyes were not so fierce,
   But with repentance wet.

But save these two is none herein
   To shatter up the soul,
And these are friends of happy Love
   Who ruin to make whole.

' The Adversary have I fought ;
   The Accuser have I heard,
But, though I mourned thereat and wept,
   I fled not for his word.

'O one I met more dark than these
  In the most holy place;
His height was as the height of Love,
  His face was as Love's face.

'But Malice in his twisted look
  With Cunning did conspire;
His words were Torment audible,
  His touch was frost and fire.

'Within these warm and narrow walks
  He leant a longing ear
The weeping of all broken hearts
  And lonely souls to hear.

'Behind him came his company,
  And many a wicked joy
From head to head went flitting past
  On mischievous employ.

'Infernal Pleasures round them ran,
  Provoking every mind;
And close behind them Madness came,
  But O too far behind!

'There many a troth-plight man and maid,
  Exchanging agony,
Smiled each to see the other pale;
  And in their van went he.

' Meseemed in heaven when golden lamps
  Love's birthday did adorn,
An evil star winked forth in hell
  And 'neath it he was born,

' To pace for aye about the world,
  Love's pair and deathly twin ;
Or if not so, it was Love's self
  Transfigured all to sin.

' Enamoured Lust and honest Hate
  Are lesser powers than he,
His very mask within the world
  Is shameful cruelty.

' I looked upon my lady's face
  And saw new motions rise ;
Her mouth was as a serpent's mouth,
  And venomous her eyes.

' My mind possessed me with delight
  To wrack her lovely head
With slow device of subtle pain,—
  But suddenly we fled.

' We saw, we turned, we fled away,
  And ask no more of God
Than now that either comes no more
  Where the other's foot hath trod.

'For if again we chance to meet
　Within this sacred grove,
'Tis he, that high malicious prince,
　Who shall between us move.

' Farewell, farewell, you happy squires !
　You ladies all, farewell !
Love grant that you may never find
　In heaven the gates of hell ! '

Faerie

UNDER the edge of midnight
  While my love is far away,
A wind from the world of faerie
  Blows between day and day.

And wandering thoughts possess me,
  Such as no wise man knows,
Death and a thousand accidents,
  And high impossible woes.

Whether now in her pastime
  She turned a little, sighed
With the heaviness of breathing,
  And even in turning died :

Or whether some cloud covers
  The lobes of the conscious brain
And all that she knew aforetime
  She shall never know again,

But her friends shall bring her to me,
  Bewildered and afraid
Lest a stranger's hand should touch her,
  A shrinking alien maid,—

Yet such distress in patience
  And faith an end may find,
And a more fantastic peril
  Moves in my dreaming mind :

None knows how deep within us
    Lies hid a secret flaw,
Where spins the mad world ever
    On the very edge of law.

Under the chance that rules us
    Anarchic terrors stir,
Lest what to me has happened
    Has never happened to her.

First love in our first meeting,
    Changed eyes, and bridal vows,
The incredible years together
    Lived in a single house,

The kisses born of custom
    That are sweeter and stranger still
Than any clasp of passion,
    And the shaping of one will,—

Was it some wraith deceived me,
    And lives she still apart
In her father's house contented,
    With an unwakened heart?

Now at this striking midnight
    Through the chink between day and day,
Has a wind from the world of faerie
    Blown all my life away?

Here am I now left naked
  Of the vapour that was she :
While the true maid 'midst her kindred
  Has never thought of me ?

For ten long years together
  Can a thing be and not be,
Till it ceases to be for ever,—
  And has this chanced to me ?

Counsels of Perfection

UNDER the trees of pilgrimage
  Two wedded lovers rode,
And made by night beneath the boughs
  Their wandering abode.

And as with little laughing talk
  They rested by the flame
Along the path of pilgrimage
  A preaching friar came.

Weary he was with many a league,
  So long the race he ran,
And speed was all the road he trod ;
Lean were his limbs and thewed with God,
  He was a mighty man.

With a high air and insolent
  He viewed those lovers' cheer,
And hailed them with a scornful voice :
  ' Sluggards, why rest ye here ?

' Know ye not well how far from here
  Your Father's house is built,
How listlessness upon the way
  Is more than all of guilt ?

' Keep ye the business of the way—
  Those high perfections three,
Obedience, virginal desire,
  And holy poverty ?

' Up, up, neglect those changing eyes,
  This shy pretended peace !
What place hath love within the law,
  Or what your joy's increase ? '

Answered the bride : ' What angry foot
  Sounds here that never paced
Where all is tranquil urgency
  And naught is toilsome haste ?

' Thy versicles upon the road
  Cry : *Nought save God can be :*
O foolishness ! without our clear
  Response : *These too are He !*

' Triple the arduous oaths ye took
  Ere your way was begun,
But we, once sworn, were sworn to all
  The darkling three-in-one.

' O Chastity !—but we were pledged
  Of old to Him alone !
O Poverty !—but save for Him
  Riches we have not known !

' O dear Obedience !—but the law
  That orders us is seen,
Love that is He and is ourselves
  And all the bonds between !

' We two were pledged to follow Him
  Where'er that guiding went,
Stripped of possession and desire
  And foreign government.

' I gave myself to love, and truth
   Therein and poverty ;
And even so, by cross and Christ,
   My lord was given to me.

' One is the road of pilgrimage
   We follow, noon and night,
Towards the house on the high hill
   In our midmost Delight.

' And when we rest beside our fire
   Because the way grows dim,
The way hath borne us, ere the dawn,
   A thousand miles to Him.

' Fair chance upon your pilgrimage
   Befall you, preaching friar ;
We rest, far distant from the End,
   Yet thou perchance no nigher.'

To Michal : Sonnets after Marriage

I

THIS you shall owe me—that your soul shall keep
Its bravery of childishness unmarred :
Awake, in love's protection ; and asleep,
By not so much as dreams of treachery scarred.

Falls, or a thistle-spike or a bee's sting,
Quarrels, and such afflictions of our dust
Shall pierce you ; but no too-quick withering
Shall age you in this heart that holds your trust.

Here shall your young eyes weep away their woe,
Your childish angers here shall have their way,
Here your intent simplicity shall show
The labours it rejoices to display,

And here shall beat unharmed, in storms of glee,
Your joyous and impetuous infancy.

II

AND so it shall be, when you come to die,
  And that strange guest, for whom no watchdogs
    bark,
Talks downstairs with our elders, though you cry
  At going out from me into the dark,—

When you must leave the attic where we play,—
  This wide clear room that on the garden looks,—
Where we have loved each other all the day
  And had our games, our picnics, and our books,—

When some old voice—which long ago was known,
  Telling our names, some pleasant voice and mild,
And bidding us be friends—shall call you down,
  Then most of all shall you be found a child,

Shrink, cry, yet bravely (by what longings sped)
Climb slowly down those last dark stairs to bed.

E

III

Apology for Neglect

PARDON, my Fair ! subdue those angry lights !
  Penitence shall with industry combine
In restoration of exacted rights
  Which, being grudged, were and yet were not mine.
'Twas but an hour—and yet 'twas thrice too long—
  That left your lonely wilful head unkissed ;
And what that can be wrought, sonnet or song,
  Shall recompense you for such gladness missed ?
Henceforward I forswear the golden lure,
  The turning wheel, the watch, the breathless pause,
The Muse, and all the covetous game unsure,
  For love's domestic and sedater laws.
Well may my purse of time in play be spent,
But never yours, nor your desired content.

IV

On her singing the Gloria

CAN that small voice assault the embanded skies
   Or, as the light air at your mouth is stirred,
   Moves all the poised creation, with the word
Shaken and shaken with remote replies?
All as a mist forms and dissolves and flies
   Before the coming—O too long deferred!—
   Of that which afar the incantation heard
And passed through worlds to answer. In such wise
   When your great sister, found on earth alone
   Mighty to speak the Tetragrammaton,
Breathed forth the *Yod* and closed upon the *He*,
   Deep in her spirit, low and small and far,
   She saw the archangel like the morning star
Poised, while the Dawn within her east was grey.

V

In her Absence

THIS is her couch, this is her very nest,
    But O the pillow is untenanted
By her incredible, dear and drowsy head,
And sleepy eyes of loveliness-at-rest ;
And easily with the first dawn I guessed
    Whose voice awoke me there—did not the bed
    Itself complain : 'Ah, whither is she fled
For whom with cunning comfort I am dressed ? '

I answer then and cry : ' O yet awhile
    Be patient, gentle friend ; she comes to-day,
        To-night your frame shall love to feel her weight.
Sleep through the sunny hours, nor more revile
    Their length than I ; she is upon her way,
        Who never yet broke promise or was late.'

VI

At the Seaside

THESE tempers and incalculable hues,
  This motion of pretended liberty,
This haste of waves that rush the shore in glee,
As children scramble for their promised dues,—
Whose is this hidden law? this impulse whose,
  So bright, so dark, so mutable, so free?
  Michal, no chance provokes you to the sea,
But kinship that creating gods infuse.

Me rather forests gladden : underfoot
Grasses and moss and many an unknown shoot
  And straying paths and straying brooks delight ;
Rough coats of bark ; innumerable trees,
Rooted and fixed and helpless ; amid these
  Corners and holes of soft indwelling night.

VII

On Domestic Government

IN the forgotten time ere mankind grew
 Out of its strife with beasts and birds of prey,
When the quick women were the first who knew
 What possible danger scented them each day,
Were they not also first to understand
 The burden and unhappiness of choice,
And, with alert evasion, subtly planned
 To leave it to men's heavier minds? their voice
Proclaimed us masters, governors, and lords,
 And kept alone the passive right to blame
If things went wryly : thus with flattering words
 They freed themselves—being still so much the same
That you (fie, Sweet !) renew their old pretence
Of my command and your obedience.

VIII

After Ronsard

WHEN you are old, and I—if that should be—
    Lying afar in undistinguished earth,
And you no more have all your will of me,
    To teach me morals, idleness, and mirth,
But, curtained from the bleak December nights,
    You sit beside the else-deserted fire
And 'neath the glow of double-polèd lights,
    Till your alert eyes and quick judgement tire,
Turn some new poet's page, and to yourself
    Praise his new satisfaction of new need,
Then pause and look a little toward the shelf
    Where my books stand which none but you shall read :
And say : ' I too was not ungently sung
When I was happy, beautiful, and young.'

In Time of Danger

I

NOW far be heavy dreams ; you hateful sprites,
  That do with many a trick of impish war
Provoke mankind to mischief, cease to mar
The sacred work, but you whom Peace invites,
Loftier divinities, with solemn rites
  At dawn and noon and day-fall, be not far
From your fair sister ; rather, while her star
Rides fortunate through heaven amid the lights
Of happy mothers, through the house let move,
  Silent and bright, the god whose aid attends
  All offices of marriage, else too poor ;
The grave companion and dear nurse of love,
  Lucina wise ; and courtesies of friends,
  In vigil—serious angels !—by the door.

II

NOW springtime is with spring o'erwhelmed, and
    white
Down the green boughs the pear tree pours its bloom
Beneath our open windows, which invite
    The entering-in of summer to a room
Decked with no other riches, by whose door
    Linger the last days of our tender Spring
Till their reluctant feet now from its floor
    A newer season exiles, mastering
With promise or threat of mightier storm or sun
    Love's leaf-twined corners and delicate buds of joy,
Over whose verdure the hot noons shall run
    And drought or tempest gather to destroy ;
But O my world, what hope for them endures
Because love's summer, as love's spring, is yours !

III

SPIRIT, who through the unfamiliar shires
    Of western England and our journeying days,
By old wrecked ships, rich fields, and thronging byres,
    Touched lately with one beauty those new ways
And her bright glance who watched them, be still near,
    Be still propitious, now her travels wend
Through high invisible counties,—in her ear
    A mightier sea than that which smote Land's End
Sounding, and over her thunder of menacing skies :
    Thou, by no other signs of presence known
Than this more brilliant laughter in her eyes,
    This cheek more darkly red, this heavenlier-strown
Abandonment to love, whose light thou art,
Thou the full passion of her abounding heart.

IV

HER house no longer knows her, nor the splendid
  Companies of bright friends who move therein,
But by her laughter and her jests attended
  She takes the ancient highroad of her kin.
Wise Habit, the long nine months' march defending,
  Goes with her to the end ; but more and more,
Upon the road from inn to inn descending,
  Each night she leaves behind her of her store.
Now fewer and more awful servants follow
  Whom one by one the gallant troops desert
Of her light mockeries ; in the night's dark hollow
  The doubtful omens shine, and none avert,
As the last smile, in the last night's rough bed,
Gleams from that childish, wise, adorable head.

V

YE who in your white house beyond the earth
  Behold the mysteries of your father Zeus ;
Sisters, if ye be sisters, of one birth,
  And be not rather one sole name our use
With diverse worship hallows,—no intense
  Grief or delight, for its own face obeyed,
Being found unfruitful ; all experience
  Being maiden and mother as thou art mother and maid,
And man's soul chiefly : Thou then, Thou, impart,
  Singular goddess, peace to the world's feud,
And with the knowledge soothe each wounded heart
  Of divine life in divine death renewed ;
Nor her forget to heal now with the balm
Of thy great Father's medicinable calm.

VI

THOU art returned, and this is safe, yet one—
    One sacrifice the infernal gods require :
What worth in thee or this if love be gone,
    Slain in the heat of that day's deadly fire?
Thou art returned, but with what hostile brow,
    What fierce and elemental enmity,
Against the heart that forced thy heart below
    Alone, yet now must share thy victory.
Sole was the conflict, parted the reward :
    Equality for ever is gone by
Between our glances ; our divine Concord
    Neglects his balance, and my scale flies high.
Death shall right all ; forget not, till that day,
Thou hast paid much, I too more slowly pay.

VII

HARK, hark, whose step is felt on our hearts' stair?
    Our truant is returning ! our best Child
Laughs out again to see us everywhere
    Amazed at his new presence : now the wild
Anarchic days are overpast and done,
    And from his sojourn in some hiddenness
Issues our Government, our elder Son,
    Our Peace, our Joy, our Hope, our Love, to bless
With old delight our newer destinies,
    To lift his brother in his young strong hands,
Mingling their breath, and with a kiss of peace
    Bestow on him his soul's most happy lands ;
But himself keep, within our hearts secure,
His rights of awful primogeniture.

VIII

ALL cruelty, all wrath, desire and shame,
   Tyranny and treachery, and what breeds with them,
   Shall Love to no sharp arrows of death condemn
But into holy fear subdue and tame
And bring into his house : as, in old fame,
   When the young Sultan of Hierusalem,
   Wearing the magical stone in his diadem
And graven on his ring the unnameable Name,
Entered his hall, his slaves were used to bring,
   For guard and glory, seven huge lions before,
Seven lions behind him ; each by a golden hair
Led to the throne of gold and ivory, where
   They all day stood and with reiterant roar
Confirmed the judgements of their lord the king.

For a Child

I. Walking Song

HERE we go a-walking, so softly, so softly,
  Down the world, round the world, back to London
    town,
To see the waters and the whales, the emus and the
    mandarins,
  To see the Chinese mandarins, each in a silken gown.

Here we go a-walking, so softly, so softly,
  Out by holy Glastonbury, back to London town,
Before a cup, a shining cup, a cup of beating crimson,
  To see Saint Joseph saying mass all with a shaven
    crown.

And round him are the silly things of hoof and claw and
    feather,
  Upon his right the farmyard, upon his left the wild ;
All the lambs of all the folds bleat out the Agnus Dei,
  And when he says the holy words he holds the holy
    Child.

Here we go a-walking, so softly, so softly,
  Through the vast Atlantic waves, back to London town,
To see the ships made whole again that sank below the
    tempest,
  The Trojan and Phoenician ships that long ago went
    down.

And there are sailors keeping watch on many a Roman
    galley,
    And silver bars and golden bars and mighty treasure hid,
And splendid Spanish gentlemen majestically walking
    And waiting on their admiral as once in far Madrid.

Here we go a-walking, so softly, so softly,
    Down and under to New York, back to London town,
To see the face of Liberty that smiles upon all children,
    But when too soon they come of age she answers with
    a frown.

And there are all the dancing stars beside the toppling
    windows,
    Human lights and heavenly lights they twinkle side by
    side ;
There is passing through the streets the mighty voice of
    Jefferson
    And the armies of George Washington who would not
    be denied.

Here we go a-walking, so softly, so softly,
    O'er the wide Tibetan plains, back to London town,
To see the youthful Emperor among his seventy princes,
    Who bears the mystic sceptre, who wears the mystic
    crown.

The tongue he speaks is older far than Hebrew or than
    Latin,
    And ancient rituals drawn therein his eyes of mercy con ;
About his throne the candles shine and thuribles of
    incense
    Are swung about his footstool, and his name is Prester
    John.

Here we go a-walking, so softly, so softly,
  Down the pass of Himalay, back to London town,
To see our lord most pitiful, the holy Prince Siddartha,
  And the Peacock Throne of Akbar, and great Timur
    riding down.

Up to Delhi, up to Delhi ! lo the Mogul's glory,
  Twice ten thousand elephants trumpet round his tent ;
Down from Delhi, down from Delhi ! lo the leafy budh-
    tree
  Where our lord at the fourth watch achieved enlighten-
    ment.

Here we go a-walking, so softly, so softly,
  Through the jungles African, back to London town,
To see the shining rivers and the drinking-place by moon-
    light,
  And the lions and hyenas and the zebras coming down :

To see bright birds and butterflies, the monstrous hippo-
    potami,
  The silent secret crocodiles that keep their ancient
    guile,
The white road of the caravans that stretches o'er Sahara,
  And the Pharaoh in his litter at the fording of the Nile.

Here we go a-walking, so softly, so softly,
  Up the holy streets of Rome, back to London town,
To see the marching legions and the Consuls in their
    triumph,
  And the moving lips of Virgil and the laurel of his
    crown :

And there is Caesar pacing to the foot of Pompey's statue,
  All scornful of his mastery, all careless of alarms ;
And there the Pope goes all in white among his scarlet
    Cardinals
  And carried on the shoulders of his gentlemen-at-arms.

Here we go a-walking, so softly, so softly,
  Up the hills of Hampstead, back to London town,
And the garden gate stands open and the house door
    swings before us,
  And the candles twinkle happily as we lie down.

For here the noble lady is who meets us from our
    wanderings,
  Here are all the sensible and very needful things,
Here are blankets, here is milk, here are rest and slumber,
  And the courteous prince of angels with the fire about
    his wings.

II. *Night Song*

SLEEP, our lord, and for thy peace
  Let thy mother's softer voice
Pray thy patrons to increase
  Freedom from all light and noise.
Hark, her invocation draws
To thy guard those princely Laws !

Prince of Fire, in favour quench
  Moonlight upon wall and floor ;
And with gentle shadow drench
  Candles entering at the door ;
Michael, round about his bed
Be thy great protection shed.

Prince of Air, lest winds rush by
  Blustering about the park
Of this night, with watchful eye
  Keep the palings of the dark ;
Raphael, round about his bed
Be thy great protection shed.

Prince of Water, if thy rains
  Must to-night prevent our dearth,
Keep them from the window-panes,
  Softly let them bless the earth ;
Gabriel, round about his bed
Be thy great protection shed.

F

Prince of Earth, beneath our tread
   And above each doubtful board
Be thy silent carpet spread ;
   Let thy stillness hush our lord ;
Auriel, round about his bed
Be thy great protection shed.

Let your vast quaternion,
   Earth and Water, Fire and Air,
Friend him as he goes upon
   His long journey, out to where,
Princes, round his final bed
Be your great protection shed.

III. *Contemplation*

ACTUALLY, child, I am a god
   Communing with you, a god :
We from our eternal stations
Behold in their infinite complexity the designs of the
    Almighty,
And among them, far away, tiny, unimportant,
Our age,
And in it, tinier, less important,
A town, a street, a cradle,
And two mortalities, each solemnly regarding the other.

On Marriage in Books

BEAUTY'S dull husband, Neighbourhood, they say,
　　When first he knew she had had a child by Joy,
Her earlier love, killed in some border fray,
　　Was tender more than wont, and to the boy
Gave food and houseroom ; then, for better aid
　　When he should come to face the world alone,
Taught him his catechism, and a trade :
　　The while his mother, making plaintive moan,
Sat in friends' parlours, to condoling ears
　　Sighing how grievous fate had left her days
Thus widowed of true marriage ; then, with tears,
　　How Love her child was learning coarser ways.
And for all this poor Neighbourhood is defamed,
Made naught of by her kindred, mocked and shamed.

After reading Hassan

I

HAROUN, Haroun, thou art gone from us, Haroun !
  And all the Arabian nights are filled with sighing,
And all the gardens of Bagdad aswoon
  In a red dream of sorrowful lovers dying.
Bountiful vagrant in our childish town,
  Hid in thy merchant robes, Islam's Commander,
Shadow of Allah, no historic frown
  Could teach us of thee any solemn slander.
No book could touch thy throne, for what thou wert
  The poets and adoring childhood made thee ;
None but the poets then could do thee hurt,
  And now, Haroun, a poet has betrayed thee.
Sons of enchantment, mourn ! for lo, from now
Haroun the Caliph wears a blackened brow.

II

And thou, no negro but a slender Moor,
   Turbaned and mailed and armed against disaster—
What child was Giafar that could be Mesrour?
   Or who was Caliph, but that he was master?
No executioner of bloody rites,
   But Haroun's friend, his warrior and warden,
And his companion through those secret nights
   In many an odorous room or lamp-lit garden!
And, more than all, thy unknown title, heard
   As of rich strangeness a more rich reflection,
' Mesrour the eunuch '—O romantic word
   Clothing thee in mysterious perfection!
Now, ere late truth tread the enchanted floor,
Return, Mesrour ; return, return, Mesrour !

To a Poet going to Rome

I

IF you shall meet them, as you doubtless may,
   Wandering some street within their heavenly Rome,
  So much like this, but lacking Peter's dome
And all the smaller churches, and they say :
' Who now among the English wears the bay ?
   Within whose mind now keeps our Muse her home ?
   Or has the world so triumphed she may come
Into no thoughts reserved her for long stay ? '

Then (our best embassy) tell them : ' There is
No age, but yours and Shakespeare's, such as this,
   Where half a hundred are with laurel crowned.
Take, of the older, these first on my tongue,
Yeats, Hardy, Bridges ; of the mighty young,
   De la Mare, Abercrombie, most renowned.'

II

Then in your turn demand of them and ask :
  ' Of all who late have joined your brotherhood,
  With whom in closest friendship falls your mood ?
With whose accomplishment ? whose present task ? '
And Shelley : ' Of all those who doffed their mask
  Of earth among us and enjoy our good,
  Tennyson, Thompson, and Rossetti brood
Nearest me, and in lyric daylight bask.'

But with a graver brow the shade of Keats :
  ' Since Blake and Wordsworth few have climbed to be
  Upon the peak whence wise Mnemosyne
Gravely to poets their vocation metes ;
  Arnold not far, nor Browning ; nearer, he
Who knew high Eros in his earthly seats.'

Shakespeare's Women

Dear Isabel,
I have a motion much imports thy good.

Measure for Measure.

WHAT word to him hadst thou to tell,
    What answer, Lady Isabel?

Or what love-token couldst thou spare
Thy prince, O novice of Saint Clare?

Would those prayer-folded hands of thine
With royal fingers intertwine?

That purposeful and austere look
His amorous ducal glances brook?

Certes, thou ill wert satisfied
To be a Duchess as a bride;

A crown and purple robes to don
As garb of contemplation;

And for Vienna's shout and stare
To change the holy fasts of Clare.

But dared thy maker part thee then
From Hero, Julia, Imogen,—

They each to partner with such mate,
Thou to right nuptials consecrate?

What more than they didst thou deserve
That from his custom he should swerve,

Nor, as his wont was, controvert
With a like husband thy desert

To them who by thy sisters go,
Posthumus, Proteus, Claudio,

Each pleased on a submissive breast?
Be thy Vincentio likewise blest!

In this thing was his justice blind?
Contented was that secret mind

When the princesses of his heart
So condescended to their part?

Sufficed it for him if he said :
' Thus, and to this man, she was wed ;

' All wrongèd lives will I accord
In giving unto each a lord '—

Bertram, Bassanio wedded thus,
Leontes and Lysimachus?

(Hardly at best he spared to tell
Of Romeo, France, or Florizel.)

Unwise to dream he never knew
What his deliberate hand would do !

Rather, while of the crowd's applause
Such nuptials served him well as cause,

He gave, to smite the eyes that see,
Passion's accustomed irony,

When each pure flame of love was lit
In the horn lantern made for it :

And how thy doom then should he spare,
O stolen novice of Saint Clare ?

On Meeting Shakespeare

I SAW Shakespeare
In a Tube station on the Central London :
He was smoking a pipe,
He had Sax Rohmer's best novel under his arm
(In a cheap edition),
And the *Evening News.*
He was reading in the half-detached way one does.
He had just come away from an office
And the notes for *The Merchant*
Were in his pocket,
Beginning (it was the first line he thought of)
' Still quiring to the young-eyed cherubins,'

But his chief wish was to be earning more money.

Cressida

FIRE catches Agamemnon's crimson sail
  And hostile arms invade the burning fleet
 Where, in the last disorder of retreat,
The shattered Grecian host without avail
Is knotted desperately; women bewail
  Already their near capture, to complete
  Whose terror one of them runs forth to meet
Love's freedom, love's imprisonment, to hail
With outflung arms and joyous eyes agleam
  Him from whose side she parted so long since—
Nigh three days—who now o'er great captains dead,
Achilles' self, Ajax, or Diomed,
  Victorious moves. . . .
                     So round the sleeping prince
Flowed the delicious future of his dream.

Borgia

THERE was no Borgia venom ; Gandia fell
    Under no sword of Caesar's ; doubtless, so.
And our cool judgements are content to know
That such a marriage group of heaven and hell
Was never throned within the Italian sell,
    Nor evil brimmed to such an overflow.
But our magnificent dreams around the glow
Of infinite wickedness compass still, where dwell
Pomps of our own undared impossible sin,
    Tumultuously potent, marvellously beautiful ;
      Where, in a superhuman mystery
      Of Christ and Lucifer, bearing those dire three,
    The Pope and the Pope's children, ramps within
The fields of Christendom a Borgian bull.

The Wars of the Roses

HO, white, white brother, tossing in the garden !
    Ho, leaping brother, tossing on the stem,
Mind'st thou the old time, before the world was silent,
    When hot and fierce we grew and pricked men's
        hearts to wrath in them ?
    When we rooted in dukes' helms, round queens' coifs
        we twined,
    Tossed upon the battles, as now upon the wind
      Tossing in the garden,
      Walks of the rose garden :
    Roses, swords, and helms a-gleam, madly all entwined !

They who walked among us, lovely lords and ladies,
    We stung them, we blinded, our scent was in their
        blood :
And life was green beneath us, and white was death
        between us,
    Gardens broke to wilderness of red rain and mud.
    Pale grew red and red grew pale, rent by the rose-thorn
    All our lovely, lordly petals trampled lay and torn,
      Tossed about the garden,
      Walks of the red garden ;
    Brake of swords a-quiver, tall maze of tangled thorn.

Like the riot and the ruin of a wild and drunken summer,
  Flowers clung upon high castles, their Houses tossed to
    doom :
White June grew all the Parliament, the Throne a crimson
    August,
    And Tower Hill was venomous in twine of mingled
    bloom.
    Horse and rider struggling—red rose-stems all about
    them,
    King and baron choking—white rose-buds there to
    flout them,
      Tossed about the garden,
      Walks of the red garden,
    England grown a garden of mad roses all about !

Ho, ho ! white brother, we tangled all the people,
  We snared the lovely princes, we dragged the kings to
    woe,
Our hearts a crimson sword-play, our smell a reeling
    battle ;
    So red roses dream o' nights, white roses rumour so.
    Ho, tossing brother, so we dream o' nights,
    Shaking in the breeze as we shook upon the fights !
      Tossing in the garden,
      Walks of the rose-garden,
    So we whisper, so we shake, so we dream o' nights

The English Tradition

HE was sixty, and gross, and good-tempered :
    He stood up in the 'bus
Bidding farewell with a general smile,
    And a wave and a word to us,
'Good-night to all you ladies ! '
    And hark, a song
Marvellously welling
    From the first throng
Of poets praising ladies
    English and dear,
    Broke over us there :
Hark, their voices sang,
    As we sat, as we smiled,
Hark, their music rang,
    Young and fresh and wild,
Tossed on the London light ;
    Lovelace, Sackville, and Carew,
    All were singing, and we too,
'Good-night to all you ladies,
    Good-night ! '

Honours

FEW chairs of dignity in England now
    The wise man covets,—not the ducal gold
Of Bedford or Northumberland, or to hold
Portfolios of statecraft and thus grow
One of the Families ; some few allow
    The impossible ambition, being not sold
    Into entire contempt but aureoled
With famous tales and spiritual show :
As, for the name of the city and our love,
    The Mayoralty of London ; then, the See
        Of Dubric, Anselm, Temple ; last, the chair,
        By Dryden fashioned and Wordsworth made more
            fair,
    Of the English Laureate ; any of these three
If a man held, he should be proud thereof.

Sub specie Aeternitatis

WHEN, shaping nations, the Creative Hand
    Moved among causes, purposefully wise,
It wrought a starry and invisible land
    And named it England : under holier skies

And in celestial darkness hid awhile,
    It waits for our discovery ; its glades
Constable saw, and Wordsworth mile by mile
    Treading its roads, beheld what heavenly shades

Changed and withdrew from mountains, moors, and rills :
    But O what deep and supernatural sound
The silent ear encounters in those hills,
    What language native to that holy ground,

Assuming all our common speech to be
    A thing of wonder, awful and divine,
Authentic accents of eternity,
    Heard here in Milton's, Blake's, or Shakespeare's line.

This is the heart of England ; it is found
    Only by such as set their souls to find
The harbours and great cities that abound
    Beyond the waters of the temporal mind.

This is the truth of England ; though she die
  On earth, a sinful and unhappy land,
She with her sisters speaks immortally
  Of all the knowledge that her eyes have scanned.

Within man's soul she dwells and hath her part,
  She is inviolable, free, and strong
For ever with perfection, since her heart
  Is filled with Humour, Irony, and Song.

On Seeing the New Moon : Palinode

I LOOKED at the young and silver moon to-night
  Sitting in heaven alone ; at a meet space
In golden agitation Hesperus shone :
Nothing between those gods and me but air.

Much was my grief to remember I oft made light
Of ancient, lovely, credulous tales ; the grace
Of the whole world approaching divinity ; the unknown
Savour of holy ritual everywhere.

Wise (and I should have known it) were they who said :
It is unlucky to see the new moon through glass,—
Procul, O procul este, profani ! who dares to gaze
On thee from the shelter of windows, O lonely, O fair ?

On the farthest reach of the soul is thy influence shed ;
And in thee the comforts of busy worlds that pass
Behold a remote far gleam upon virginal ways,
Behold thee, a goddess, a huntress, arrowed and bare.

By streams, or on the high hills, or in windy brakes
Of the woods shall thy maids or those who love thee sing ;
Or at worst, in the streets of the town, to the open sky,
Their casements be opened and their entreaties poured.

Therefore, Divinity, now will I bring thee cakes
Broken at cross-roads, and this verse I bring,
And an oath that in time to come if this moon go by
The windows shall all be wide and thou be adored.

At a Tubè Station

OUT of deep tubes and tunnels
  When I to open air
Up a round shaft am carried
Or climb a spiral stair,
The calm evening twilight
Catches me unaware.

In the deep tubes and tunnels
That cross and slope and wind,
In catacombs and caverns
And subways of the mind,
Journeying goes my spirit
Where is no peace to find.

Roaring upon its trackway
My swaying will returns,
Where crowding thoughts, as strangers,
Press on their hid concerns,
While in a blaze above them
My arc'd self-knowledge burns.

Within my earth deep-hidden,
Shrieking, the tumult goes,
From darkness into darkness
Plunging without repose,
Piercing black tubes and tunnels,
Or checked where knowledge glows.

But here the open twilight
Breaks on me unaware :
The pavement, the tall houses,
The trees and the fresh air,
The carts, the folk, the voices,
And all things everywhere.

The faint moon in the heaven,
The sun with his gold fleece,
The dust beneath my footfall,
In one great flood of peace
Flow down their silent channel
And deepen and increase.

With Time and Space for borders
Lest any wave disperse,
Flows forward, without eddy,
The holy universe,
As to its own broad music
Moves a high poet's verse.

But I stand up within it,
In separation clad,
As they who once in Jordan
A dry footing had,
Or he who trod in Ganges,
Woe-stricken Ladurlad.

The Bruised Heel

ALL the heat, as they float over earth, of infectious
stars,
Hatching tyrannies, plots, rebellions, giant wars ;
All prisons, and innocent lives that find the street
And the cloud their prison ; all listless heavy feet ;
All cancers with twisted root that shall never be whole,
And cancerous slanders draining a true man's soul ;
All scaling leprosy eating the face away,
And scaling avarice no content shall stay ;
All hearts that are sick in the sleeplessness of night,
And sick in the conflict of dawn ; all grudge of delight
In surly households ; all frenzies of day or dream
Till alike the heavens of earth and spirit seem
Pale and drawn by the pain of the deep abscess at the core
Of Being—
         O heart, if this indeed were no more
Than a hurt, than a rub by the way, than a prick in man's
heel
Which a day's rest soothes and his health no more shall
feel,
Nor his foot delay, nor his mind be wracked, so long
His infinite way is, his joy in the way so strong !

To the Protector, or Angel, of Intellectual Doubt

GODS many and lords many be
In houses of divinity,
But o'er those houses, in all lands
Builded with laying on of hands
And rites of high purgation, sent
From God, their full accomplishment,
Over all altars and all roods
What solitary spirit broods?

Protector, your due praise receive
From us who in your strength believe
And by your purity are clean!
For, O you doubt of all things seen,
How but by you shall men come in
To the delights of Faith your twin,
Your younger and fair sister? Who
Dares set division 'twixt you two,
Making intolerable trial
With harsh assertion, harsh denial,
Speech that was never meant to be,
Of your still breachless comity;
Planting a hedge of uncouth words
And angry slanders, till the birds
Of vision only can go free
From hers into your liberty.

Yet Truth knows naught to reconcile
In your exchanged prophetic smile,
For what glad games betwixt you please
Her ardours and your honesties !
And each hath rest-chamber assigned,
Guests of the hospitable mind
Which makes of questions and of vows
One household, as yourselves one house.

Through mortal cities where we go,
Spring of refreshment, clearly flow ;
Beneath their firm foundations deep
Let your destroying waters creep,
And their stability unfix ;
Or let your rains between the bricks
Wash out the mortar ; try if there
Of all the walls the past held fair,
Fitting the stones with arduous pains,
Aught indestructible remains.
Or with a subtler toil surprise
Our slothful too-accustomed eyes :
Work, work beneath that show ! till, while
We go about the streets, your guile
This apparition quite undoes
Of buildings multitudinous ;
Till all the mighty towers that were
Settle, and sway, and disappear,
Softly dissolve and gently fall,
And your broad waters take them all !

Your ceremonial doth prepare
A place for Love's doctrinal chair ;

Beyond your river, broad and bright,
His halls and colleges of light
Shine in each courteous heart ; all fond
And happy moments lie beyond
This world's mistrusted fields of sense
Moated by your deep waters, whence
A bridge of arched amazement leads,
And large discovery succeeds.
Yours is that soil, yours is that air,
Of rich and antique foster where,
Incredulous but faithful, we
Enter into humanity.

On all the body's roads we tread
Be Love's the wine, but yours the bread !
Your wheaten loaves for ever be
Conjoinèd with each ecstasy
Of new delight, and wheresoe'er
Through meadows green and cities rare
We travel, daily let us make
Our meals of your provisioned cake.
Or if that highway plunges in
Jungles where monstrous beasts of sin,
With their fleshed cubs of brute desire,
Beneath the hot boughs do suspire,
And in the place of the good sun
Is light from fiery Phlegethon,
O skilled in hill and jungle craft,
Our true shikari, loose your shaft,
You from all dread malaria free
By healthful incredulity !

All vast Illusions' conquering shade,
Preserver from opinion, raid—
Maya, Chimaera, vapourings
Risen from the breath of men, whose wings,
Mightily spread, veil all his sky
But shred to mist when you are nigh,
And leave us to clear knowledge ! Keep,
Shepherd, your flock of silly sheep
From panic rout ; let no lust thrive
In us, nor ogreish shadow drive
With a huge bludgeon of black fear,
Nor frenzy dwelling in us here,
Our feet the ancient piggish way
Of steep Gadara ; mild and gay,
Preserve us from all hurtful food,
Clover and else, in hungry mood
Eagerly swallowing, to find,
Too late, the pain of the blown mind.
When the whole world is full of gales,
Of rumours, flatteries, and tales,
When the mob's breath or Caesar's drives
Into one blast all minds and lives,
Close, close about us, while that storm
We seek to buffet, be your warm
Cloak of consideration drawn,
And lead us to a quiet dawn !
Be, where the slanting roads divide,
A peace, a shelter, and a guide !
Spur through our inner night and morn,
Another Palomides, sworn

To seek the Questing Beast ; pursue
Down the old pathways and the new
Its hideous noise of barking hounds,
Till in the mind's unhallowed bounds
At last its wrath be slain or thralled :
You, to that high vocation called,
From Mecca of the idols come
To Islam, thence to Christendom,
And bound in turn to that last coast
And city of the Holy Ghost,
Who, as his well-belovèd say,
Hath driven opinion clean away.

For you too, in the Faith made fair,
Have put on angelhood, and there
Called your disciples, few but skilled,
To the devotion of your guild :
Not with your candid raiment marred,
As the hot grasp of Abelard,
Ere loosed to counter Bernard's blow,
Caught it and tore it, *Yes or No,*
But lightly wrought and worn at ease
In those expanding sanctities,—
Choosing now this, now that to be
Aim of your joyous irony,—
As when some happy lover lights
With sudden disbelief his rites
Of adoration, and at once
Retires, approaches, loves and shuns
The sweet face of his mistress, pleased
To be of mere devotion eased,

And graver for the vision seen
Of the lacked joy that might have been.

Ah, if such gaiety were all!
But Faith must everywhere need all
Your aid; foul enemies she knows,
And you must save her from her foes!
Not Superstition: her, 'tis true,
Faith took, when she was far from you,
To be her waiting-maid, and now,
Where'er she looks, that stupid brow
Must gaze beside her! but let be,
Think 'tis your sister's charity
To keep her, who would elsewise make
Marriage with man he could not break
Save, driven at last beyond his force,
By atheistical divorce.

Darker the ills that Faith endures,
Which naught but your swift brightness cures:
O learn'd in exorcisms, lay
Two ancient spectres of the way;
Her own void apparition she
Beholds,—carrion Hypocrisy,
Swelling and black, with noisome breath,
Laden with all its past of death,
Its mist of mockeries, its gloom
Wherein religion stifles, whom
Soon to destroy, O come, beloved
Salvation,—as of old you moved
And armed with many a dangerous gift
The fierce disdainful hand of Swift!

Nor, saving so the head of Faith,
Despair to meet that lighter wraith,
Which is your image and your grief,
Utter and intimate Unbelief;
Who chills your delicate sweet heart
With its frigidity,—your art
Of subtle exploration spoiled,
As those first darting barques were foiled
Who sought what Northern road might be
Into the well-known warmer sea,
By creek and channel, gulf and bay,—
Lo, naught but ice about them lay
And in that cold they perished. Keep,
To save us from that final sleep,
Some highway, narrow, twisting, deep,
Amid a silent frozen world !
O when the very heavens are curled
Frozen above us, when the earth
Is a bleak certainty of dearth,
When all our homing instincts freeze
Within us, to black crevasses
Are turned the ancient tender bays
Of love and friendship, when in stays
The soul's confinèd ship delays,
And never, never can get free
From loveless arctic prisonry,
Then, then, be with us, and redeem,
Let the ship feel your moving stream,
And by that flow, discovered new,
Open the bergs, and bring us through !

For this, be your high saints implored,
Whose images we have on board,—
He of the Twelve, wise infidel,
Who did all tales of Truth repel,
Till, proved to every questing sense,
It shone, Its own best evidence,
Then filled at once his faithful place ;
She who, being wholly full of grace,
Was left not foolishly without
Fine tides of intellectual doubt,
Sceptic interrogations, she
Who, saying ' How shall this thing be ? '
In that one asking did retrieve
The pale credulity of Eve ;
Yea, and a mightier name than hers
Within this royal worship stirs,
For who but you began long since
To tend the anguish of your Prince ?
When slipping, scourged, and nigh to fall,
Was't not your whisper : *Is this all ?*
First lifted, stayed, and held him ?   When,
Bound on the massive cross of men,
In the full passion of His ill,—
When, ere the Sacred Heart was still,
The Sacred Brain endured the shoot
Of dereliction, wert thou mute ?
Didst thou not then, ere Faith could turn
Through tears her comfort to discern,
In that great night, leap forth to clear
A space to breathe about Him there ?

Did not your arrows of sharp doubt
Find all the priestly mockers out
And pierce the brag of Pilate when,
Showing Him Caesar's power of men,
He showed Him all the solemn thrones
That ever judged a prisoner's moans?
Faith succoured Him when struck to death,—
But who save you can succour Faith?

Witchcraft

NOT for cattle or gold,
   Not for houses or land,
I go to the evil Sabbath
   On this night, and stand
Under the icy throne
   To take the icy vows
And be accounted one
   Of our Father's house.

Our Father who wert in heaven,
   A lonely road is Thine ;
Hardly after long travel
   Shall we reach to our design,
Hardly by prayer and vigil
   Into Thy presence come,
Hardly by that last gate
   Of fiery martyrdom.

Many shall stand by Thee
   Upon this Sabbath night,
In vengeance or love or gold
   Seeking for their delight ;
High leaps up in their heart
   The flame of earth's desire,
But quench in Thine own elect
   That too-long smouldering fire !

Over the whole world
  Through the streets of many a town
The seven deadly Sins
  Go lightly up and down.
But from their sweet delays
  Set Thou Thy children free ;
'Tis Thou, not they, we seek ;
  Father, draw us to Thee !

Envy and Anger and Lust
  Are half the kin of Love,
But Thy great throne is lifted
  All lesser thrones above :
Whose sole joy is to see
  Love weep and bleed anew.
This, this is all our prayer—
  That we may aid thereto.

All the proud Asian kings
  Who have loved torment well,
All sweet malicious tongues,
  How far Thou dost excel !
O Terror ! O Cruelty !
  O Hate ! O Anguish of Joy !
Make our hearts one with Thine
  To ravage and destroy.

On the cross at the world's end,
  Where that Other hangs,
There, Thy back to His back,
  Endurest Thou Thy pangs :

H 2

There on our perfect longing
   Nail us with spines of ice,
And break our mortal hearts
   In the great sacrifice.

Poor and hungry and bare,
   His elect saints go by;
Poor and hungry and bare
   Must Thine adepts draw nigh.
To see our lovers weep
   Under our word or kiss—
Naught else will we ask or have;
   Our Father, grant us this !

O cold, cold, cold,
   The piercing wound shall be
When in an utter loathing
   We are made one with Thee,
Beyond all hope for ever
   Of knowing love again
Save with its core of malice
   And weeping eyes of pain.

The Purchase

SMALL and red and goggling with anxious eyes
   At the full shop windows, the folk, and the carts in
      the street,
Clutching a stolen penny in one fat hand,
And torn with doubt between this or that other sweet
For look and size and taste I see myself stand.

' No one shall have my penny,' I hear myself say,
And watch the greedy, unpleasant child slip in
To the central bazaar, where all may ask and have:
They sell everything there, and he for his pennyworth sin
Asks with hot breath and panting voice: O brave!

' God shall not have my penny, this clever God
They talk of,' I feel myself thinking; ' he may be there,
Behind the chocolate boxes, or just outside;
I have never seen God, I don't know God, and I don't
      care;'
The penny is gone, and he runs away to hide.

Is it I that watch? is it I that am choking with haste
Over the moment? surely 'tis I that walk
Serene in the world, and Love comes down the street
With all my princely friends, and we stand and talk.
Is it I that hatefully hide and gobble my sweet?

Gracious the world appears ; a small fat boy
Goes carefully past,—what have I to do with him ?
' Now you know where the pennies are you can get one
    each day,'
I feel him thinking ; my love's bright face grows dim,
And the talk of my friends is farther and farther away.

And the great Republic closes to one dull lane,
One ugly door, and towards the door I go,
Thinking how nice but how short the taste was, and why
The man in the shop was so stern, and if they know,
—Slinking and licking my fingers and ready to cry.

The Parrot

WHILES, when I sit alone, I hear my soul,
    At the far other end of the room that is me,
  Head cocked aside, in vacant persistency,
Trying over some word it has caught from me, some toll
Of my daily tongue, some little habitual phrase
  That was plaintive in me, but ironical and unkind
  From that iron beak, some phrase as *It 's not that I mind*
Or the silly *I think he needn't* . . . And then of the days
I dream when my journey must come and I remove
  From the streets of Time to the shires of Eternity,
  Those counties sprinkled with towns, and the heavenly
    sea,
And the gardens of peace, and the high strong house of
    Love.
Will this then come with me also, and still with its air
  Of inquisitive cunning go practising over again
  All it has learnt from me here, and its talk be plain ?
Will it fly through those gardens and clamour and haunt
    me there
Among the trees, and all shall know it for mine ?
  For mine ? or for me,—loosed to my doom in that sky ?
  Here a cage and a cover I have, but there the birds fly ;
Soaring and sinking and resting in joy divine,
Each with its own call, happy, busy, and glad,—
  There a dove, there a lark, there even a ravaging hawk,
  But only this parrot for me with its hideous squawk,
  . . . Then I cover it up, lest the dream should drive me
    mad.

The Other Side of the Way

I PROMISED about this time to call at a house
  On the other side of the way, which is heaven, and see
If Immanuel is there and will finish his business with me.

It's the pleasanter side : the tumble-down houses here,
  The frowsy people, the mud, the raucous calls,
  Are pretty bad when I look at those shining walls.

It seems silly to walk on this side when I might be there.
  I jostle and splash and am hardly fit to be seen ;
  Only—the road is up in between.

The barriers stretch right along without opening or break.
  The workmen there have their faces turned away,
  And if I speak never listen to what I say ;

Unless I try to go by, then a hard voice says
  ' No crossing here, sir,' an all-but-violent hand
  Thrusts out to push me back, so here I stand.

It must be a long while ago that I promised to call.
  Too far to go back : besides, it's getting dark
  And the street-lamps show no more than the merest
    spark.

Night in this neighbourhood ! night with these neigh-
    bours ! these fat
  Slimy faces ! these lean greedy smiles ! What supper,
    what room
  Should I find here—O what dreams in the gloom !

But if I go on,—what to do? the poles stretch along
  Unbroken as far as I see, and every yard
  May take me away from that house down a road still
    barred.

Yet there the thing is! there's heaven! and there are
    its gay
  Bright tenants, but they don't look, and this horrible
    smoke
  Has got into my lungs; if I try to call out I choke.

No good to turn back, no good to go on, no room
  To cross, and no hope to find room, and all the unlit
  Side turnings here going steeply down to the Pit.

A Dream

NO more in any house can I be at peace,
　Because of a house that waits, far off or near,
To-morrow or (likelier) after many a year,
Where a room and a door are that shall fulfil my fear.

For last night, dreaming, I stood in a house and saw
　Softly the room door open, and one come in,
　Its owner, and as round the edge his evil grin
　Peeped ere he passed, I knew him for visible Sin.

Unwashed, unshaven, frowsy, abominable,
　In a green greasy hat, a green greasy coat,
　Loose-mouth'd, with silent tread and the smell of the
　　goat,
　He stole in, and helplessness stifled rage in my throat.

For this was he who came long since to my heart,
　This was he who entered the house of my soul long ago ;
　Now he possesses imagination, and O
　I shall meet him yet in some brick-built house, I know.

He shall come, he shall turn from the long parch'd street
　　he treads
　For ever, shuffling, hand rubbed over hand unclean,
　Servile yet masterful, with satiate spleen
　Watching his houses, and muttering of things obscene.

He shall come to my flesh as he came last night to my
    dream ;
  Eyes shall know him as soul and insight have known ;
  Though all the world be there, I shall stand alone
  Watching him peer and enter and find out his own.

Noisier he shall not move, nor loudlier speak,
  Than the first sly motion of lewd delight in me
  Long since—which then I shall know none other than
    he,
  Now visible, aged, and filled with monstrous glee.

Therefore now in terror I enter all houses, all rooms
  Enter in dread, and move among them in fear,
  Watching all doors, saying softly ' It draws more near
  Daily ; and here shall it be in the end,—or here ? '

Tartarus

UNDER my mind, so near I stand to the edge,
　　It crumbles, and I, from ruin barely saved,
Fling myself back, as at once, without shelf or ledge,
All life into nothing suddenly drops away.

Where was I walking, where ? . . .
The firm world stretches without me, of things and men ;
Common delights that sudden gap repair ;
Nothing in everything once more is vanishèd.

Higgledy-piggledy, through my brain, my thoughts,
In many alien lands born, of many minds,
Under far ascetic poles, upon sensuous ghauts,
In temperate meadows, but all here naturalized,

Hurry ; unending that dim crowd stretches away.
My body is linked to the earth and cannot cease ;
In death, but not destruction, shall end its day.
In body and mind all 's sure, all 's help at need.

Yet deep within me, wherever I stand or go,
I feel now the suction, the drag, the desire of the void
To swallow for ever the spirits of men, the flow,
Towards chaos ever-thinning, of souls disjoined.

Sick, sick from that shudder's last throes, I am shaken ;
　　pale
Must I walk and troubled hereafter, ever at point
To see in a room, in a stream, in a friend's face, and quail,
The farther gate of hell that gives on the void :—

The gulf, whence all the kingdom, the glory and power,
Suffices, yet hardly, to save us, lest we should sink ;
Nothing, that presses against us each hour, each hour
Held back by the full-stress'd might of heavenly things ;

The choice and sole dwelling of those who, dropping self-
tossed
From the City whose streets in salvation their fellows
walk,
Drift, dying for ever and ever, where, first of the lost,
Lower and lower and lower Beelzebub falls.

Judgement

FAREWELL, my Day, yet ere thou art quite departed,
Say, invok'd by this prayer, this last good-night,
How shall I find, by what sign know thee again,
In eternity entering when I behold thy dawn?

Thou and thy brothers there, equal in worth,
Children of Time (old riddle!) timelessly gathered,
Wait, sleeping in God till I come, then rise upon me,
Each a witness, a word, a sign, a judge in session,
Each with his passionate hour,—and which then was
    thine?

The first kiss of happy morn? the gesture that fits
Beauty, some epiphany perfect of perfect love
(Such is thy fortune, Fair, and such thy grace,
In a world insignificant thou significant wholly)?

Or, Day of bewilderment, shall I behold thee scarred
And my accuser, saying, ' Thus I avenge
Upon thee my wrongs, my wounds, and with mine
    Creation's ' ?

Merciful then, O Day, for this poem I bring,
This repentance, this reparation,—such thy due
From me, to whom be merciful then as now
Granting sweet sleep, as I bid thee good-night, my Day,
Thou who art Christ, Christ who is more than thou.

In Time of Strife

ETERNAL Justice, who dost all things weigh,
In those strict balances thou keep'st above,
Against the scale whose only load is Love
Sitting, a child, with fiery darts at play,
Ere yet thou puttest in our deeds to-day
Charge them with living metal till they prove
Able to bid thy needle cease to move
And to its rest thy beam exactly sway.

Then, not too heavy with excess of fear
And anger, nor too airy, rash, and light—
Either deserving naught of thee but thence
Worthless to be cast out—let them appear
Under thy smile poised equal with that bright
Exalted and perpetual Innocence.

A Meditation on the Three Theological Virtues

GODDESS, by threefold ceremonies adored :
    On bloody altars in the infernal ways
  Where sad ghosts walk, and many a lost life strays
Darkly, and all-but-hopeless Death is lord ;
And in the upper world,—where, long implored,
    Oracular prophecy no more delays
    To cheer thy faithful worshippers,—with praise
Of song and broken cake and wine outpoured :

Thou in the last and holiest mysteries
    And in thy heavenly session hast no name,
      Title or rites, but only his who draws
      All souls in thee, O motion of his laws,
    From worlds of daylight or of Stygian shame
To dwell where wholly thou and thine are his.

For a Picture

*Of the Madonna teaching the Divine Child geometry
by figures drawn on the sand (Merejkowski)*

STRAIGHT lines and circles, triangles and squares,
  With exact finger on the sand she draws,
   Marking how each new truth from its own cause
Demonstrably arises, and prepares
Place for more truth to follow ; so, she bares
   The sacred and inevitable laws
   Which are his nature and design, and awes
Him with his own perfection : the Child stares
Rapt at each new device, while gravely flows
   The mighty theorem,—rapt into a fine
Ecstasy at the argument prepared,
And darkly now himself already knows
   The union of dimension, ideal line,
Inclusive number, and the circle squared.

I

On my Friends coming to hear me Lecture

WHY from their own concerns should they be
    brought?
Surely no wit or subtle cunning delves
Into the strata and deep seam of thought
    They could not mine more deftly for themselves!
Mere self-oblivion then? must it be so?
    One perfect moment of pure charity
Fiery about the figment and the show
    Of thought and sound and gesture that is me?
Happy if so their souls with Godhead kiss;
    And be subdued, my proud revolting heart,
To be the negligible cause of this
    Rather than hold their fancies by your art.
What lovelier office can befall a friend
Than so to serve the acceptable End?

On arriving anywhere in time for anything

HOW good the Universe can be !—What now?
How many fail this moment from their assigned
Fixed hour ! is the Universe then blind
To them, or does it turn a hostile brow
Upon their needs and to me favour show,
   Having a variable and lawless mind,
   Benevolent now and now again unkind,
Luck in its depth as on its surface? No,
But if the myriad wills that live and work
   In its will, so fall that this hour is free,
Foiling the contradiction we feel lurk
In all things, shall not the Universe rejoice
   Through its whole mind, with its least child, with me,
In this appointment kept, this fulfilled choice?

Christmas

' LET us go a journey,'
　　Quoth my soul to my mind,
' Past the plains of darkness
　　Is a house to find
Where for my thirsting
　　I shall have my fill,
And from my torment
　　I shall be still.'

' Let us go a journey,'
　　Quoth my mind to my heart,
' Past the hills of questing,
　　By our ghostly art,
We shall see the high worlds,
　　Holy and clear,
Moving in their order
　　Without hate or fear.'

' Let us go a journey,'
　　Quoth my heart to my soul,
' I shall thrive never
　　On the world's dole.
Past the streams of cleansing
　　Shall a house be found
Where is peace and healing
　　For my aching wound.'

By the streams of cleansing,
  By the hills of quest,
By the plains of darkness,
  They came to their rest.
As the kings of Asia,
  They went to a far land ;
As the early shepherds,
  They found it close at hand.

When they saw Saint Joseph
  By their ghostly art,
' Forget not thy clients,
  Brother,' quoth my heart.
When they saw Our Lady
  In her place assigned,
' Forget not thy clients,
  Mother,' quoth my mind.

But my soul hurrying
  Could not speak for tears,
When she saw her own Child,
  Lost so many years.
Down she knelt, up she ran
  To the Babe restored :
' O my Joy,' she sighed to it,
  She wept, ' O my Lord ! '

Easter

WAS there not one, when in the upper room
   The women broke crying, ' He is gone—he is gone,'
Who felt beneath a blast of heavier doom
   His soul go down?   Not Peter, royal John,
Admirable Thomas, but perhaps unknown
   Bartholomew, Judas (not Iscariot),
Who at the tale of the Rolling of the Stone
   Knew himself chosen, by a dreadful lot,
To grace and strife and immortality,
   And blessed but perpetual martyrdom,
Uttered one last lost cry, ' Ah, not to me ! '
   Even as from air he saw the Arisen come,
Nor felt within him the black terror cease
Even as around them fell the greeting, ' Peace ' ?

Saint Michael

THERE was a motion within Deity,
  And the first Seraph lived, saw, and became
One cry through all his nature and his name,—
Micha-el : Who is like God? Thence to be
Began the hierarchic mystery
  Of spirit : where, though he be first in fame—
  Goldenly-helmed ; thrice winged, thrice ringed with
      flame—
Yet each of his Angels is hardly less than he.

But all his Angels and he, gathered into one
  Fire, as a lantern high upon the mast
    Of the Admiral's vessel, shine ; and in their track,
With night-watch set and guards at every gun,
  Float through the ocean of the unknown vast
    The twelve huge ships of the moving Zodiac.

Saint Mary Magdalene

WHAT great Apostle,
  When the Christ rose,
Met with him secretly
  In the garden close?
Fast ran Saint Peter,
  Fast ran Saint John,
When they heard the rumour,
  But our Lord was gone.
Only in the morning
  He was earliest seen
By a weeping spirit,
  Mary Magdalene.

Once in a glory
  To my heart he came,
Born of a maiden,
  With love for his name ;
But what bitter passion
  On myself for tree
Hath his bounty suffered !
  Now deep in me,
Silent, unmanifest,
  Hiding his power,
During a time and times,
  Waits he his hour.

High Imaginations,
  Wait, sad and still,
Till a sudden rumour
  Your desire fulfil.
But, O blessed Magdalene,
  When the first dawn
Shines across my spirit
  From that garden lawn,
Watch with me, speak with me,
  Blind me with tears,
When angels fall silent
  And Himself appears.

Saint Stephen

ALL Doctors and Confessors,
  Martyrs and holy Souls,
Lighten my path of darkness
  With your aureoles,
When I come to die.

Three times shall I perish :
  Once when my will,
Loathing itself for learning,
  Learns a heavenly skill
To bring itself to die.

Once when my tired body
  Death touches with his hand,
Wrapping all my movements
  In a ghostly band,
And to earth I die.

Once—O Soul too happy
  If it probe the gloom
Of its last deprival
  In the mystic tomb,
Where the elect must die ;

If it find the inmost
  Final mystery
Of dying even from Heaven,
  And that death is He !
If it come to die.

Pray, all you Confessors,
  And, O crowned with palm,
Stephen and all Martyrs,
  That I find your calm,
When I come to die.

On the Sanctissimum

I. The Real Presence

WHEN the young Church was robbed of her Adored,
    Eager and innocent her longing mind
Mean after mean to ease her heart designed
With his pretended presence for reward.
For first in haste his sayings she explored,
    But yet he came not ; soon the cross she signed
    In court or catacomb ; then, for still she pined,
Shaped thereupon the image of her lord.
Last, in a passionate rush of memory,
She sank, she cried : *This, surely this is he,*
    He newly come, Himself become our food.
Divine deception ! . . . had his tenderness
Not foregone time and outrun her distress,
    Murmuring : *This my body, this my blood.*

II. Crux Mundi

NOT thee, ourselves on thee for cross, O Lord,
   Herein we see ; feeling the whole world hang
  Distraught, and knowing not whence comes the pang,
Nor how its hands and feet are bound with cord
Of hate and nailed with longing to the abhorred
   Tree of its grief, nor that the word which rang
   (In its cheated ear) of pleasure only sprang
From its own pain's delirium : now, O stored
With sap of a new spring, grow with us one !
That, then thy perfect crucifixion,
   Teach us ; which known, the healing virtue works :
Dying, we have no strength except we die.
   In dreams of a green tree what madness lurks,
But O what blossoming beauty in the dry !

III. At Communion

STILL must the implacable road lie dark and bare
   Before me, all the turnpike dues being paid
   And right direction followed, which obeyed
Should have led long since unto thy presence?   Where,
My God, is any house now but despair?
   Whose is the guilt if still the frost invade
   The hoped-for Spring, and check the piercing blade
Of love? what love, when warmth deserts the air?

Deserts?—when all thy fellows thou canst see,
   O foolish heart, bright with a noble cheer,
     On all sides round in new perfection drest!
Thou couldst not miss them, Lord, therefore not me!
   Thou art in them, then here, O therefore here!
     Though still thy hid communion serves me best.

IV. At a Procession

OUT of the now redeem us into Now!
  Out of the moment bring us to the End,
  Which is not ending merely, but the blend
Of all the process and the event, for thou
Dost in this moment—hiding but the how
  Besought by all philosophy—expend
  Thyself in act, and so dost ever mend
This now with thine Eternal. In this show
Thy wedded contraries go softly by :
  Moving, thou mov'st not ; changing, dost not change.
    Thou art, and all is that would else but seem.
Delicate contemplation ! Thou draw'st nigh,
  Thou passest, thou. All time we have for range,
    Yet time that is not Now were but a dream.

Satisfaction

WHILE now upon the bank my engineers
  Of purpose, gathered in no easy rest
But quarrelsome talk, disputing and distressed,
Behold their frustrate bridge and broken piers
O'erwhelmed by those high-flooding deaths and fears ;
  And by them waits—leaning upon his breast,
  Spirit, in him as he in her sole blest—
Thwarted Imagination, whose sharp jeers
Mock at their toil . . . suddenly all is gone ;
  Their voices in silence, in wide air are lost
  Their gestures ; now, nor ford nor bridge being crossed,
I wander here, at peace with myself and alone,
  From this clear hill seeing, o'er a gentle tide,
  My futile works,—lo there on the other side.

To a Publisher

WHEN the divine John out of heaven, great sir,
    Saw the Free City over earth expand,
Lighting the shadows of the things that were,
And all that here was soured or fell to waste
    In winds unmanageable, bringing to bland
Maturity and seasonable taste :

Therein twelve guilds he saw, the twelve great wards,
    Twelve principles of being, twelve clear gates
Each to some mystery none else affords,
Each with its fair of high solemnity
    Whereat with show and feast it celebrates
Its past eleven moons of industry :

Farmers who long with vigil tend the soil,
    Sowing divinity and reaping it,
And in due harvest carry home their spoil,
With song and merriment accomplishing
    The heavenly year, and with new-conscious wit
That Corpus Christi fully hallowing ;

Another day the bold discoverers,
    Heroes and saints, since heaven itself is dim
With distance and with innocent danger stirs
Their hopes, come riding inland to address
    The gains of their devotion unto him
Who touched the bottom of the bottomless.

K

But O what dawn, sir, shall behold our state,
  Our carnival, our triumph, our good cheer,
When through the streets from our in-pouring gate,
Under observant galleries everywhere,
  We range the City, and at last draw near
The dais and the high mayoral chair.

Company there by company shall pass by,
  Each with its tossing banner,—and our own,
Not least in that exalted pageantry,
Bright with its golden legend, *Dominus
  Illuminatio*, and the triple crown,
And you, and I perchance ; and over us

Shall all the songs who here on earth were books,
  Whom we, according to our wealth, made free,
Flutter like cupids, and with gentle looks
Present us to their lord and principal,
  Good craftsmen, prudent in our mystery,
Not slothful here at task, not slow at call.

Around that seat throng the high Presences,
  The Archangelical Letters, who first bore
The separating Word in their degrees :
They chief who when the Unnameable was named
  Grew to the boundary of Space, the Four
Who are the walls wherein the whole is framed.

And all the sounds who serve man's tyranny,
   Misshapen, broken, running to and fro
Upon our meanest business, we shall see,
Attending on the happy silent Word,
   Whom here we hardly did as footboys know,
Nor save for our own needs could they be heard ;

The drudges of Desire, the scavengers
   Of metropolitan Possession, pale
Sons of poor tailors, cooks, and labourers ;
Lean words that found so little happiness,—
   Vagrants of talk or styed up in the jail
Of pedants' lore,—and never knew success

Until some fortunate poet drew them forth
   Out of that misery, charged them with power,
Re-bathed them in their ancient pristine worth,
And through his meditation they again
   Escaped to their own land, whom in his hour
They sing to have lived on earth nowise in vain.

They have their life, but at what cost of death,
   Out of such dark impassioned moment born
As when young Browning met Elizabeth,
Or, turned from watching on Niphates' head,
   Milton lamented blindness, or forlorn
Catullus mourned above his brother dead !

And we who could not so refresh our night,
   Who are no Shakespeares, nor no Campions we,
Yet shall go up among them, nor the flight
Of those deft wings shall there neglect our love,
   Who gave them once a second liberty,—
The poets gave them heaven, we earth to rove.

They, of earth's fame still shyly covetous,
   And still with nothing but their love for fee,
Petitionary came, and found with us
Shelter and shipping for what voyages
   To ports of mind beyond the public sea
They risked their hopes on and their health's increase.

Patrons and printers, what we had we gave,
   Blessing them with devotion and desire
Meetly to serve,—Caesar, Southampton, grave
Linnell and bright Lorenzo, many a king
   For some sole gift of lodging or attire
Remembered at his dynasty's sunsetting ;

And many a copying monk who in his cell
   With gayer colours touched a poet's line
For love's sake than a preacher's, drawing well
Plated Aeneas helming forth the fleet
   Of Trojans from coifed Dido, with the fine
Walls of a Gothic Carthage at her feet.

And many a darker mind who in his day
   Set up the types with weary eyes and slow
And heavily for food re-told the lay
Of the spent Mariner or of Isabel,
   But in his heart felt light from that strange woe
Trouble the common thought he knew so well.

These shall be counted, these with lifted brows,
   Bright with the virtue of that ancient care,
Shall pass ; and all the princes of our house
Who mightily did once themselves expend
   Upon creation—Taylor who loved Clare
And Keats, and Moseley who was Milton's friend ;

And many a learnèd critic of our guild
   Who kept in secret purity his mind,
Watching the stars' discretion,—when to build
A house of reputation for some child
   Of verse or prose, and when to turn unkind ;
And now walks bravely, free and undefiled.

And as each soul or song one moment gains,
   Fronting Phoebean deity face to face,
His central pause, the universal strains
Prolong his note around in harmony,
   And the whole City, bowing towards his place,
Reverberates his name eternally.

For there in turn republican all are
   Our masters, and we theirs ; so interchange
The hierarchical degrees afar ;
Waxing and waning, dwindled or increased,
   In order as in light, all spirits range
The whole ascent, now topmost and now least.

Heaven shall not lack interpretation ; all
   The heavens, by our great mystery and art,
Shall become common and reciprocal ;
Yea, without us eleven guilds should be
   But a dumb joy, we are their singing part,
Their publication and epiphany.

And if at all in any than the rest
   More of Immanuel's delight can be,
Are not the Carpenters his friends confessed
And we his later fellows,—the two trades
   He followed, through his thirty years and three,
Of wood and words,—nor his skill ever fades.

Shall he forget the intimate sweet word
   Breathed to his Mother when they needed wine,
Or the sharp edge of thought which like a sword
Destroyed Apollyon, his own prayer, or that
   Seraph who ran before him for a sign
And is for ever the *Magnificat*?

But O than these a gift more marvellous
   He to our great assembly doth commit,—
His rich significant silence ; unto us
He is the depth where music doth rejoice :
   Let the rest hear his praise and cherish it,
We are the praise he speaks, we are his voice.

Only at last, when is no more to tell,
   And our disparted union dies away,
Lost in our solitudes innumerable,—
As some sole thrush who, amid garden trees
   In the last light of the now sunless day,
To one whom evening from his labour frees,

Brings peace and joy and news of love to be,
   So to each spirit a remote sweet call
Marks closer stirrings of divinity
Than any high publicity of dawn,
   The stars shine in a farther heaven, and all
The City in great stillness is withdrawn.

Last Thoughts before Sleep

WHO shall awaken first,—the saucy quean,
 The mother of my soul, august and mild,
The passionate lover, the fixed friend, the keen
 Woman of affairs, the absurd and humorous child?
Who of them all shall come, ah! who shall come
 When first her mind feels morning, when she feels,—
Sweet, when we feel ourselves again become
 What now is slipped from me, slips from me, steals
I cannot tell where . . . But now, my mind is so clear,
 You are so warm and close, so warm I lie,
That now is the time to think great things; with you near,
 I feel such thoughts as I never had go by . . .
Such deep things . . . and presently tell you what I knew,
So warm and close, so close and so warm are you.

Printed in the United States
99490LV00001B/227/A